Living in Thailand

Living in Thailand

New Edition

TEXT BY WILLIAM WARREN
PHOTOGRAPHS BY LUCA INVERNIZZI TETTONI

Thames & Hudson

Page 1: Detail of a gold-and-lacquer scripture cabinet, Jim Thompson Collection.
Page 2: Gilded stucco, mosaic and mirrors adorn the walls of Wat Rajabopitr, Bangkok.
This page: Guest rooms overlooking a lily pond, The Anantara Resort, Hua Hin.
Following pages: The poolside area of Villa Royale, Phuket.
Page 8: Dining pavilion, designed by Ed Tuttle, in a private villa, The Amanpuri.
Page 214: A design of mother-of-pearl inlay showing mythological animals and
traditional Thai patterns.
Page 215: Wall mosaic representing the sacred bodhi tree, Mandarin Oriental Dhara Dhevi.
Endpaper: Detail of Thai Lü folk-art temple mural, The Rachamankha.

First published in the United Kingdom in 1988 by
Thames & Hudson Ltd,
181A High Holborn,
London WC1V 7QX

www.thamesandhudson.com

This new edition 2006

British Library Cataloguing-in-Publication Data
A catalogue record for this book is available from the British Library

ISBN-13: 978-0-500-51332-3

ISBN-10: 0-500-51332-5

Printed and bound in China

Contents

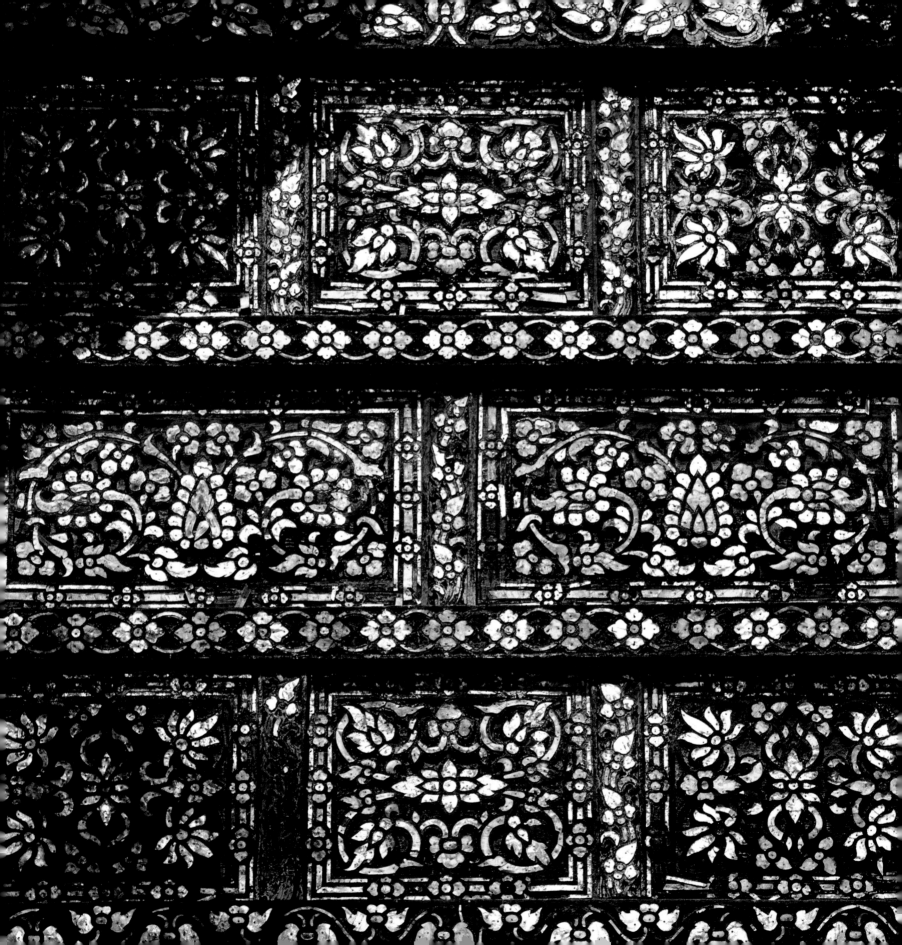

Introduction

A variety of influences have been artfully blended over centuries to produce the unique phenomenon we call 'Thai style'. This can be found in both religious and domestic architecture, and in countless decorative details that define this distinctive culture.

The special style that defines a culture is born of many elements. Thai style, so vividly revealed in its art and architecture, is the product of a distinctive landscape, a skilful use of varied influences and a history unique among the nations of Southeast Asia.

Thailand today is a multi-faceted kingdom of 50 million people, most of them Thai in the ethnic sense but many of them Chinese, Malay, Indian, Khmer and other races that have played important cultural roles. It is also a kingdom of contrasts— new and old styles coexisting, now and then subtly merging in ways that often enchant, sometimes surprise and occasionally bewilder an outsider.

Buddhist temples adorned with ornate decorations, baroque fantasies at once witty and otherworldly, rise on crowded city streets. During lulls in the din of traffic, one can hear the faint music of bells and the soothing sound of monks chanting. Along rivers and canals, motorboats speed past plain but striking traditional houses with graceful peaked roofs that are silhouetted against a pale, tropical sky. In the market places of the far north, amid tape recorders, plastic pails and other artefacts of the modern world, one will find tribal people in bizarre costumes of medieval splendour. The King of Thailand now lives in a wholly Western palace, adorned with communications antennae through which he keeps in touch with his far-flung projects around the country. However, within the same compound reside the royal white elephants, treasured symbols of monarchy since the first rulers began to shape a national identity.

Uniting these disparate elements like a slender but surprisingly tough thread is a spirit unmistakably Thai. To fully appreciate it, to comprehend the complex creation of 'Thai Style', it is necessary to go back to the kingdom's earliest days.

About a thousand years ago, in the opinion of most scholars, the first sizeable groups of Thais began to migrate southward from the Chinese province of Yunnan to the region they would make their home. They came seeking greater independence for the distinctive culture they had developed over many centuries and they came, too, like most of the world's migrant peoples, in search of better land and room for expansion. They were to be notably successful in both quests.

The country now known as Thailand offered the newcomers wide topographical variety and a wealth of natural resources. The mountainous north was rich in hardwood timber trees, an easily available source of building material, and watered by numerous streams and rivers. The far south, a narrow isthmus stretching like a long finger to the Malay states, enjoyed a plentiful supply of seafood from the seas off its two coastlines as well as rare ores and precious stones. The north-eastern plateau, semi-arid today, was then thickly forested and amply supplied with water. Most alluring of all was the Chao Phraya River basin, a self-contained geopolitical unit and one of the world's most fertile rice-producing areas, where most of the great Thai kingdoms were to rise in future centuries.

Earlier groups were also drawn to these riches. Archaeologists have found evidence of prehistoric settlers going back to the Palaeolithic Age, 500,000 years ago, in places as widely separated as Chiang Rai in the north and Kanchanaburi, west of Bangkok. The most significant development occurred on the Khorat Plateau in the north-east, where, beginning around 4000 BC, a remarkable culture rose and flourished until shortly after the beginning of the Christian era. Known as Ban Chiang, after the small village where the first discoveries were made, its people cultivated rice, wove textiles and

made pottery decorated with stylish red geometric designs. Particularly intriguing to historians is the fact that by around 3000 BC—far earlier than any previous estimates, perhaps as early as anywhere—they had learnt to produce some of the world's first bronze and copper tools, which later developed into highly sophisticated items of daily use and personal adornment.

Pending further discoveries, an aura of mystery still clings to the people of Ban Chiang and their subsequent fate. Did their methods of clearing land lead to their impoverishment, driving them down from the plateau? Did they pass on any of their skills to later inhabitants? The answers are a matter of conjecture; all we know is that their culture came to an end around AD 200 and at about the same time, other performers appeared on the stage of history.

Two of the most important were the Mon and the Khmer, both of whom had considerable influence on the development of Thai culture. The former, establishing a kingdom known as Dvaravati, settled in the western half of the Chao Phraya River valley, while the latter made their home on part of the north-east plateau and in modern Cambodia. Buddhism was introduced from India, according to legend, around the 3rd century BC by missionaries of the Emperor Asoke, and Indian influence remained strong for several centuries, especially on Buddhist art in the south of the country.

By the 12th century AD, the Khmers were the most powerful group, ruling from the mighty temple city of Angkor. Their empire covered much

BOTTOM LEFT **An old engraving of the Bayon temple at Angkor. Khmer rule once extended over much of modern Thailand and wielded a powerful influence on Thai architecture and culture.**

ABOVE **Painted pots from the late period of the Ban Chiang culture, which rose in north-eastern Thailand around 4000 BC and declined shortly after the start of the Christian era.**

BELOW **A bas relief at Angkor Wat featuring Thai mercenaries marching with the army of Khmer King Suryiavarman II. This is one of the earliest depictions of Thais, who at the time had migrated in large numbers to the region where they would later create a culture of their own.**

of present-day Thailand and the remains of their *prang*-centred temples, rich in Hindu symbolism, can be found scattered through the north-east and in the central plains as well. However, Khmer power was weakening and the time was ripe for later arrivals to assert themselves and create a style of their own.

The first Thais formed city-states in various parts of the far north, in places like Chiang Saen, Chiang Rai and Chiang Mai, united for a time in a loose federation known as Lanna Thai but never exerting much power outside the region. Other groups left the mountains, however, and by the 13th century there were substantial Thai populations in the plains and even—somewhat mysteriously—as far south as Nakorn Sri Thammarat. At Sukhothai, near the northern edge of the plains, they probably outnumbered the Khmer overlords and around 1243, three of their chieftains united to establish the first truly independent Thai kingdom.

Sukhothai lasted less than 200 years, but during that time it was the scene of extraordinary cultural achievements, among them the evolution of the Thai concept of kingship, the invention of Thai writing and the beginnings of Thai styles of art and architecture. Its prosperity and freedom from unfair constraints is celebrated in a famous inscription dating from 1292 during the reign of King Ramkhamhaeng, still learnt by every Thai schoolchild: "There is fish in the water and rice in the fields. The lord of the realm does not levy a toll on his subjects for travelling the roads, they lead their cattle to trade or their horses to sell, whoever wants to trade in elephants, does so; whoever wants to trade in horses, does so; whoever wants to trade in silver or gold, does so."

Sukhothai today is filled with hundreds of ruins, all of them religious buildings. These monasteries, or *wats*, reflect borrowings from a wide variety of cultures, principally Khmer, Mon and Singhalese. But they also display a number of uniquely Thai features like the graceful lotus-bud tower that later became the spiritual symbol of the kingdom and highly original images of the Buddha in bronze and stucco relief. Chinese potters—supposedly brought into the country by King Ramkhamhaeng—introduced the art of making fine ceramics and Sukhothai wares were exported in large quantities to Indonesia, Borneo and the Philippines.

Due to a custom forbidding the use of durable materials like brick and stone for any but religious buildings, nothing remains of Sukhothai's palaces

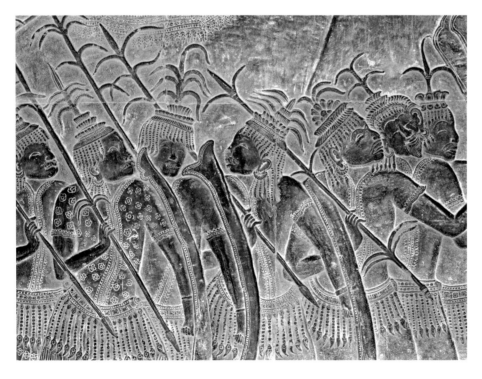

BELOW **A bas relief at Angkor Wat featuring Thai mercenaries marching with the army of Khmer King Suryiavarman II. This is one of the earliest depictions of Thais, who at the time had migrated in large numbers to the region where they would later create a culture of their own.**

or domestic houses, all of which were built of wood or bamboo. From fragmentary mural paintings that survive in temples of the north, however, it seems probable that the houses were simple structures with steep thatched roofs, raised off the ground to afford protection from floods and wild animals, and displaying few if any non-functional decorations. The palaces were larger, to judge from the area they occupied, and may have been adorned with woodcarvings appropriate to their royal residents; but again, they were basically plain with unpainted wooden walls hung on a frame of stout poles.

Thai architecture evolved further in Ayutthaya, a new kingdom that arose in the Chao Phraya basin during the 14th century, and so did the fortunes of the Thai people. From a small town with rough mud fortifications, Ayutthaya grew in both size and splendour. By the late 17th century, it had a population of more than a million and a skyline of flashing temple spires and elegant multi-tiered roofs overlooking miles of crowded waterways lined with houses.

Sukhothai *wats* had been relatively subdued except for their stucco decorations. By contrast, those of Ayutthaya at its peak were magnificent with gold leaf, coloured tile mosaics, elaborately carved wooden gables, vast murals and doors ornamented with delicate gold-and-black lacquer paintings, incorporating designs often borrowed from Khmer or Indian sources but given a particular flavour that turned them into something Thai. Since its rulers adopted the Khmer concept of divine kingship, palaces underwent a similar transformation and

many features of the temples appeared in their decoration. Starting in the reign of King Narai (1657–1688), they were also made from brick, which added to their imposing appearance. The first Western-style buildings appeared in the Ayutthaya period as well, one of them a palace with European decorations in the summer capital of Lopburi where a French embassy was received by Narai.

Domestic houses, of course, were simpler but apparently had the airy raised platforms and practical construction that we know today. Simon de la Loubère, who came in Narai's reign, described the majority as being made of bamboo and unusually portable: when three houses happened to block the king's view of a proposed firearms demonstration, "the proprietors had taken and carried them away with their furniture in less than an hour".

Bangkok, established as the seat of government by King Rama I in 1782, was originally modelled after Ayutthaya, which was totally destroyed by the Burmese 15 years before. In its first 50 years or so, it was almost wholly Thai in appearance, a conscious

ABOVE **An 18th-century French engraving of Ayutthaya on the Chao Phraya River basin. Ruling the kingdom for four centuries, the city became one of the largest and most cosmopolitan cities in the area.**

effort to reproduce the glories of the old capital through general layout and specific buildings. Early travellers commented on its splendid *wats*, its mile-square Grand Palace compound, the densely-packed double rows of floating shops that lined the Chao Phraya and the network of Venice-like canals that served as streets.

The evolution of the central Thai domestic house—with its distinctive curved roof ends and panelled walls—was now complete and hundreds of them could be seen throughout the city, some of impressive size and workmanship while others were simple in the extreme. Joseph Conrad, who came as a sailor in the late 19th century, described "an expanse of brown houses of bamboo, mats, of leaves, of a vegetable-matter style of architecture, sprung out of the brown soil on the banks of the muddy river. It was amazing to think that in those miles of human habitation there was not probably half-a-dozen pounds of nails".

But even when Conrad wrote, this water-oriented phase of Bangkok's history was drawing to a close, doomed by the rapid growth of its population and new concepts of urban life. Alone among the countries of the region, Thailand

never had an alien culture imposed on it through European colonisation. Nevertheless, Western influence penetrated with increasing force, making itself felt first in the capital and then, at a somewhat more gradual pace, in more remote parts of the kingdom.

Roads appeared and with them shops and houses of solid construction in foreign styles. As the canals lost their vital importance as arteries of communication, more and more of them were allowed to silt up and eventually became streets to accommodate the growing number of vehicles. Much of what remained of the distant past either vanished during the building boom that started soon after the Second World War or retreated to seldom-seen byways hidden in the shadows of a brand-new skyline. The transformation was so great, both in the city and outside, that a casual visitor today may find it difficult to find the elements that were once so distinctive.

Closer inspection, however, reveals the tenacious strength of Thai style. In its purest forms, it survives through the fanciful temples and the more subdued yet elegant classic houses, both of which continue to be built. It can be found as well in many structures that remain from the later 19th and early 20th centuries—more than may appear at first glance—outwardly so foreign in appearance yet still responding to landscape, climate and social demands in a peculiarly Thai way. Finally, it is present in numerous contemporary homes, in which traditional concepts and modern building materials are combined to create new versions of Thai style.

Sukhothai

Sukhothai—where a group of Thai chieftains united and established their first capital—ruled for less than two centuries between 1238 and 1368. Yet it was the scene of remarkable developments, both political and cultural. By the reign of King Ramkhamhaeng the Great (1279–1300), the ideal of a paternalistic monarchy had evolved as well as an active trade with foreign countries. The Thai alphabet was devised here and many distinctively Thai ornamental and architectural features first appeared on its numerous Buddhist temples. No trace remains of Sukhothai's domestic houses and palaces, which were constructed of wood and bamboo.

OPPOSITE **A seated Buddha image in the ruins of Wat Mahatat at Sukhothai.**

ABOVE **This stucco relief in Wat Phra Sri Mahathat Chalieng shows the famous walking Buddha, one of several features of religious art that originated during the Sukhothai period.**

Ayutthaya

Ayutthaya, which overpowered Sukhothai in the 14th century, was the capital of the kingdom for nearly 400 years. At its peak in the 17th century, it was filled with magnificent palaces and temples and had a population estimated at more than a million—larger than London at the time—among them many foreign traders. The city fell to the Burmese in 1767, after which most of its treasures were looted or destroyed by fire.

OPPOSITE **Wat Phra Ram in Ayutthaya was founded in 1369 and completely restored in 1741.**
ABOVE **The three *chedis* of Wat Si Sampet.**

Rural and Urban

ABOVE **House boats and rice barges on the Chao Phraya River at Ayutthaya are still a prominent feature of river life.**
RIGHT **Thai-style buildings surrounded by water are among the many features, both old and new, at the Ancient City just outside Bangkok.**
OPPOSITE **The Chao Phraya River at Ayutthaya, with the Khmer-style tower of Wat Chaiwattanarah rising mysteriously in the background.**

For much of Thailand's history, and in rural areas today as well, water has been the dominant natural feature of life, nourishing the essential rice fields and providing an important means of communication. In the central plains, the principal artery is the Chao Phraya River and on its fertile banks have arisen three capitals—Ayutthaya, Dhonburi and Bangkok—along with countless smaller communities. Canals stretch far into the countryside and serve as roads linking various villages.

With more than six million people, Bangkok today is some 45 times the size of the next largest city in Thailand. In its early days, life was centred on the river, overlooked by the mile-square Grand Palace and also by most of the foreign legations and commercial establishments. Towards the end of the 19th century, the city began to move away from the Chao Phraya, across miles of former rice fields, eventually acquiring a modern skyline of towering office buildings to replace the old exotic one of gilded temple spires.

ABOVE **The Erawan Shrine, honouring the Hindu god Brahma, lies at a major intersection in modern Bangkok. The curving tracks above are those of the mass-transit Sky Train.**

RIGHT **The Chao Phraya River cuts through the capital city of Bangkok. It is still a busy artery of communication for many of the city's residents.**

Thai Forms

The particular elements that comprise Thai style range from the obvious to the subtle, from architectural features that transform a building to design motifs that require a practised eye to discern.

anyone coming upon them.

Recognition of Thai style, as this suggests, is easier than sober analysis. Its varied components tend to be elusive and hard to pin down with precision, like the hot, sweet and sour flavours of the country's celebrated cuisine, each making its presence felt in ways so subtle it is difficult to say where one stops and another begins or exactly when an outside influence—Chinese, for instance, Indian, Khmer, even Western—loses its original form and evolves into something distinctively and uniquely Thai.

At every turn, though, in highly Westernised cities like Bangkok as well as in the remote countryside, the eye is constantly finding memorable manifestations of the phenomenon in creations large and small, humble and exalted. For outsiders, these may come with the first glimpse of a Thai *wat*, or monastery, those dazzling structures that prompted Somerset Maugham to remark: "It makes you laugh with delight to think that anything so fantastic could exist on this sombre earth." Their steep, multi-tiered tiled roofs, graced at the ends by slender, refined finials known as *chofahs,* or 'bunch of sky'; their gilded spires rising gracefully to dizzying heights; their complex decorations that range from entire walls of inlaid glass mosaic to doors and windows adorned with black-and-gold lacquer paintings—all contrive to come together into a coherent whole that is undeniably spectacular and yet also, in a mysterious way, profoundly serene.

It may come, too, in other forms: in lacquered cabinets, doors or betel-nut boxes inlaid with

PAGE 26 **A modern interpretation of an ancient Lanna motif by Angkarn Kalyanapongsa in Wat Sri Khongkham, Payao.**
ABOVE **An ornate *howdah* used by high-ranking northern Thais when travelling on elephant back. The removable shade is made of woven cane while the frame is wooden, with lacquer and deer horn decorations.**

The sinuous elegance of graceful curves contrasting with the formality of rigid lines and geometric patterns; an occasional note of grave restraint and formality—almost but not quite amounting to severity—relieved by moments of exhilarating artistic abandon that suggest surrender to a burst of irrepressible joy; now and then a sudden touch of what can only be called pure whimsy, sometimes expressed through eccentric forms so unexpected and lighthearted they bring an involuntary smile of serendipitous discovery to

intricate mother-of-pearl designs; in the abstract patterns formed by both brightly-hued tiles on a temple or palace roof and the simple thatch on a farmer's house; in the sense of colour and pattern that transforms floral wreaths given as offerings into minor works of highly perishable art. Items for ceremonial or royal use display Thai designs in their most refined manifestations—low tables and chairs, ornately carved and often gilded; fine lacquer boxes and footed trays; gold or silver nielloware, a craft for which the southern city of Nakorn Sri Thammarat is still celebrated; Bencharong, a multi-coloured enamel ware with Thai patterns, first made in China exclusively for export to Thailand; and richly brocaded silks flashing with gold threads.

Equally, however, the simplest of traditional household utensils may display it in such forms as rice baskets and fish traps woven into a wide variety of shapes, each serving a specific purpose yet having an innate beauty that lifts them out of the merely utilitarian; a coconut scraper in the form of a crouching animal; a water dipper that is at once practical and elegant; water jars either starkly plain

or glazed and decorated with mythical animals; a colourful *pasin*, or sarong, woven on a home loom and worn by a village girl.

Most of these have evolved over centuries, sometimes inspired by other cultures, sometimes purely indigenous. Fine glazed stoneware, including sea-green celadon, was exported during the Sukhothai period in the 13th century, while pottery is still found in the same shapes as those produced 600 years ago in Ayutthaya. Similarly, the basic designs of baskets and textiles have changed little over the centuries. But Thai style is by no means stagnant. It continues to make itself felt, often in unexpected places. Flamboyantly, it is present in the primitive artwork that adorns *tuk-tuks*, or motorised tricycles, that ply the streets of Bangkok, the lorries and tour buses seen on highways, and the long-tailed motorboats that speed up and down rivers and canals. At the same time, contemporary artisans are adapting it to create works that serve modern purposes yet reflect a sensibility that is inherently Thai.

LEFT **A graceful celadon water container in the shape of a mythological swan from the northern kiln of Phan, near Chiang Rai (J Shaw Collection).** BELOW **Wooden coconut graters, carved in the form of rabbits. To use, sit on it as you would on a stool and scrape the coconut against the metal. Such graters, which come in various other forms, were once found in many rural households.**

ABOVE **Windows with gilded stucco decorations on the Dusit Maha Prasat in the Grand Palace, dating from the reign of King Rama I (1782–1809).**
RIGHT **Tiered roofs and gilt-mosaic finials known as *chofahs* on the Amarindra Vinitchai Audience Hall in the royal palace compound.**

Early Bangkok

Multi-tiered roofs are the most memorable feature of Thai temple and palace architecture, and dominate the landscape. The first royal buildings in Bangkok, founded as the capital in 1782, were conscious evocations of those that lay in ruins in Ayutthaya. Of particular splendour was the mile-square Grand Palace on the Chao Phraya River, which contains some of the finest examples of traditional Thai art and architecture.

Lanna Thai and Ayutthaya

The earliest Thai city-states were established in the north, in a loose federation called Lanna Thai. During the Ayutthaya Period (1350–1767), Thai style reached a peak of elegant craftsmanship in many parts of the kingdom.

OPPOSITE **Gold-and-black lacquer window of the library at Wat Saket, Bangkok. The library (late 17th or early 18th century) was moved from Ayutthaya to Wat Saket by King Rama I. The panel decorations show foreign merchants, a theme that originated in 17th-century Ayutthaya and persisted until the early Bangkok period.** THIS PAGE (*left top*) **Model of a temple in the Lanna Thai style; painted wood with glass inlays (Banyen Folk Art Museum, Chiang Mai);** (*left bottom*) **An 18th-century model of an Ayutthayan** *vihan*, **or assembly hall; wood, painted and gilded. The model clearly shows certain features of Ayutthayan architecture such as the boat-shaped podium, called a** *thawng-samphao* **(ship's hull), and tiered roofs (Wat Machimawat Museum, Songkla);** (*left*) **Window of the** *vihan* **at Wat Phantao in Chiang Mai. The Makara arch above the window is gilded woodcarving with inlaid mosaic and the motif, also found at Sukhothai, is of Indonesian (Srivijaya) origin; the barred window shows Khmer influence.**

Decorative Arts

Wood and stucco, glass mosaics, patterned textiles, gleaming lacquer covered with delicate paintings in gold—these were some of the mediums through which the traditional Thai artisan expressed his imagination. Motifs recurred over the centuries, sometimes with subtle variations, always with an exuberant sense of colour and an eye for detail. Similar designs, for instance, are found in both Ayutthayan and early Rattanakosin (Bangkok) decoration, though in the latter they have become far more profuse, usually covering every part of a surface in rich but somewhat rigid geometric patterns.

Thai Pottery

The earliest pottery found in Thailand dates from prehistoric times. During the Sukhothai period (13th to 14th centuries), beautiful glazed wares with distinctive Thai designs were made and exported to several countries in the region. Ayutthaya (1350–1767) produced only unglazed pottery, though large quantities of porcelain were imported from China.

ABOVE **Glazed stoneware with fish designs, produced in Sukhothai kilns in the 14th century; diameter of the plate on the left is 23.5 cm.**
RIGHT **Fish plate with border motif of creeping plants; diameter 31 cm (Surat Osathanugrah Collection).**

LEFT Unglazed stoneware jar from a kiln at Si Satchanalai near Sukhothai (Surat Osathanugrah Collection).

ABOVE (*top*) Water jar with lid and stand in baked clay, from the late Ayutthaya period; height of the jar is 50 cm (Neold Collection); (*bottom*) New celadon water containers from the Northern Kiln of Kalon (J Shaw Collection).

Furniture

Traditional Thai homes, particularly of the lower classes, contained relatively little furniture beyond a few storage containers and woven reed mats for sleeping. More elaborate pieces were found in palaces and in houses belonging to wealthier members of society, as well as in Buddhist temples where the scripture cabinets and ecclesiastical chairs were often works of high art that employed such skills as woodcarving, lacquer and inlaid glass mosaics. With increasing Western influence, European furniture began to appear, sometimes decorated with Thai motifs, sometimes adapted to Thai customs, as in the case of low dressing tables.

OPPOSITE **A scripture cabinet** (*left*) **and a 19th-century Thai dressing table (both from the Neold Collection).**

LEFT **Three decorative details from traditional Thai furniture. The one at the top, from a library cabinet in the Lopburi Museum, includes angels probably inspired by European influence in the late 17th century. In the middle detail, from an early Bangkok period bed, similar figures have become characters from Thai mythology. The third shows part of a Thai table in the collection of Khun Chaiwut Tulayadhan.**

BELOW **A traditional seat for monks (Neold Collection).**

RIGHT **A selection of Bencharong ceramics (Prasat Museum Collection).**

BOTTOM **A Thai lacquer tray holds a collection of crystal bowls from the reign of King Rama V. These were made in Europe to Thai design specifications.**

OPPOSITE *(top left)* **Lid of a ceremonial container;** *(top right and middle left)* **Made-in-China Bencharong ware (Jim Thompson Collection);** *(middle right)* **Detail of *laithong*, or washed-by-gold, design;** *(bottom left)* **Detail of a silver bowl from northern Thailand;** *(bottom right)* **A betel-nut set in nielloware.**

Elegant Rattanakosin Utensils

The first half of the Rattanakosin Period saw a continuation of the love of colour and intricate decoration that had characterised Ayutthaya. Artisans, often under royal patronage, produced a wide range of fine traditional crafts for use in palaces and aristocratic homes. Others were produced abroad with designs being supplied from Thailand.

Furnishings of an Old Northern Household

Plentiful natural resources, together with a variety of artisan communities, have traditionally made northern Thailand a centre of such crafts as woodcarving, lacquerware, silver, ceramics and ivory work. In Chiang Mai, separate villages, each specialising in a particular art, once stood just outside the city walls. Today, they have been absorbed into the urban area; even so craftsmen tend to group in the old areas and pass down skills to the next generation.

OPPOSITE **A selection of lacquerware from northern Thailand (Neold Collection).** THIS PAGE (*top left*) **Lacquerware containers;** (*top right*) **Northern silver bowl with embossed design (Dhara Dhevi Collection);** (*middle left*) **Footed silver bowls used for offerings (Dhara Dhevi Collection);** (*middle right*) **A sword and collection of handles for ceremonial knives;** (*bottom left*) **Ceramics from the north (J Shaw Collection);** (*bottom right*) **Silver betel-nut set in a lacquer container (Dhara Dhevi Collection).**

ABOVE **A typical *lan kruang jak san*, as shops selling kitchen utensils and other household goods are known, in Nakorn Phanom near the Laotian border.**

Everyday Utensils of Rural Life

Following techniques and designs handed down for generations and utilising easily available local materials, Thai villages still make most of the goods needed in their daily life. As in the past, these simple items not only serve a specific purpose but also often display a striking elegance of form.

THIS PAGE **A selection of the items used in daily life in rural Thailand, all handmade from local materials:** *(top left)* **Hats from the north;** *(top middle)* **A ladle made from a coconut;** *(top right)* **A basket for carrying chickens, commonly used in Chiang Mai;** *(middle left)* **A container for rice;** *(middle right)* **A container for keeping freshly-caught fish. Such containers are found throughout the country;** *(bottom left)* **Containers from the north for storing glutinous rice;** *(bottom right)* **Water bottles made from gourds.**

45

RIGHT **A selection of contemporary celadon wares produced by the Mengrai Kilns in Chiang Mai. This ancient art of fine ceramics began in the Sukhothai period and still survives.**

OPPOSITE **In the two pictures at the top, workers at the Mengrai Kilns are placing wares in the biscuit (moderate heat) kiln and applying chiselled decorations to pots. The other pictures show the dyeing, spinning, weaving and tying of *ikat* cloth, a fabric in which the warp or weft threads are tie-dyed before being woven.**

Continuing Crafts

Most of Thailand's traditional crafts continue to be produced in various parts of the country, stimulated in recent years by a new appreciation of their beauty and utility. Jim Thompson, an American who settled in the country after the Second World War, created an international market for Thai silk, and a foundation established by Her Majesty Queen Sirikit promotes a wide range of village crafts. Moreover, modern designers are finding new ways to use the old techniques for striking creations to decorate contemporary homes.

Street Art

Mythology as well as the Thai love of colour distinguishes many of the decorations that adorn otherwise mundane trucks, taxis, buses and motor tricycles on city streets as well as on boats and buffalo carts. Among the legendary creatures shown on these pages—all of which can be found in traditional temple mural paintings as well—are voluptuous mermaids, mythical lions, dragons and the half-human half-bird *kinaree*. Such decorations originally served as magic protection and in many cases, still do.

OPPOSITE **This elaborate design was found on a boat in Narathiwat.**

ABOVE **A selection of intriguing art work that can be seen on Bangkok vehicles.**

Spiritual Abodes

BOTH PAGES These spiritual
abodes are from various
locations around Thailand and
show styles ranging from simple
to ornate. Displayed on each are
typical offerings such as floral
garlands, food and other items.

A feature of almost every Thai residential or commercial compound is a small structure that houses the spiritual guardian of the property. Usually elevated on a pole to eye-level, these are often simple wooden replicas of the traditional domestic dwelling but may also, especially in cities, be elaborate affairs of coloured cement modelled after royal or religious structures. Other spirit houses are placed near sacred trees, in caves and at particularly dangerous places on roads where accidents have been common. All are kept supplied with regular offerings of incense, flowers, food as well as doll-like figures of people and animals that represent spiritual attendants.

Not all such abodes are erected for guardian spirits, however. Many are dedicated to Hindu divinities such as Brahma and Siva or to legendary human beings who have become part of popular folklore. Devotees of such shrines come to pray for a wide variety of things, among the most popular being success in business, better health and a winning number in the national lottery. The usual offerings are made at the time of the first visit and grander ones if the wish is granted.

OPPOSITE **A ceremony marking the installation of a new spirit house. Brahmin priests in white costumes preside over the more prestigious of such ceremonies, chanting prayers and supervising the assorted offerings, which on the occasion shown includes flowers, fresh fruit and cooked delicacies. Brahmin rituals also play an important role in numerous royal rituals, such as the Ploughing Ceremony held annually across from the Grand Palace to mark the beginning of the rice-planting season.**

LEFT **Offerings at a spirit house in downtown Bangkok. These figures, both human and animal, are presented as symbolic attendants for the resident spirit.**

Traditions

Though often outwardly simple and perfectly adapted to local conditions, the traditional Thai house displays many symbolic features that vary from region to region. Royal structures may be more ornate but follow the same basic plan as those of ordinary people.

In the first decade of the 20th century, an English painter named P. A. Thompson passed a pleasant day touring Bangkok by boat, then still the most convenient way to explore Thailand's capital. On one suburban *klong*, or canal, he came across a number of houses "of the typical, low-country type", which he described as follows:

"A platform of teak planks is supported on piles, six or seven feet above the level of the ground, and approached by a ladder leading down into the klong. Opening on to two sides of the platform are little houses, also built of teak, with graceful gable ends curving upward to a sharp point. In the city the roofs are tiled, but here they are generally thatched with attap. If the people are very poor, perhaps they will only have a platform of bamboos, and the walls of the house will also be of split bamboo and attap interlaced. The platform is often gay with flowering shrubs, amongst which brilliant butterflies flit about. It forms the courtyard, from which it is only a step up to the floors of the houses. The sleeping-rooms are at the back, but in front and open to the platform are deep verandahs, in which the family live during the day."

Every foreign visitor to Bangkok who put his thoughts to paper commented in awe, and often at considerable length, on the city's dazzling Buddhist temples, which reveal Thai style at its most ornate. Somerset Maugham's reaction was characteristic:

"They are gorgeous; they glitter with gold and whitewash, yet are not garish; against that vivid sky, in that dazzling sunlight, they hold their own, defying the brilliancy of nature and supplementing it with the ingenuity and playful boldness of man. The artists

who develop them step by step from the buildings of the ancient Khmers had the courage to pursue their fantasy to the limit; I fancy that art meant little to them, they desired to express a symbol; they knew no reticence, they cared nothing for good taste; and if they achieved art it is as men achieve happiness, not by pursuing it, but by doing with all their heart whatever in the day's work needs doing."

Most travellers also found space for a description of the impressive double rows of floating shophouses that lined the Chao Phraya River and reminded them of an Asian Venice. Thompson, however, is one of the few to dwell in any detail on the classic domestic Thai house—less spectacular than the religious buildings, to be sure, but nevertheless a remarkable architectural achievement in its own right, displaying a style both practical and uniquely Thai.

The structure Thompson admired—with its steep roof, its spare but elegant decorative features, its prefabricated panelled walls and its rooms opening on to a breezy upper platform—was the Central Thai house, probably the best known of at least three distinct styles in various parts of the country. Whether all have evolved from a common origin is a matter of scholarly debate. Some leading experts on the subject believe each developed independently out of different influences, despite similarities in construction. Others, who favour the evolutionary theory, point to the existence of certain architectural features on houses and Buddhist temples in the southernmost provinces of China, where large communities of ethnic Thais still live.

Though summers are humid, winter temperatures drop to freezing in this part of China and the houses are thus designed for warmth. Those of the ethnic Thai are raised from the ground and made of wood or bamboo, with steep roofs that are thatched or tiled. The more permanent wooden ones usually consist of a large room with only a few small windows for air circulation. A single stove placed near the entrance serves for both cooking and heating the house; mats for sleeping are arranged near the source of warmth. Trapped by the lack of ventilation, the smoke has stained the unpainted walls black and the atmosphere is generally dark and faintly claustrophobic, almost the opposite of the popular conception of a Thai house elsewhere.

What identifies the structures as Thai and distinguishes them from Chinese houses in the area is the elevation from the ground—even though in some cases it may be less than a metre—and the steep roofs, sometimes multi-layered with expansive overhangs to protect the interior from both rain and sun. Some of the bamboo houses, in fact, are raised quite high, with the open-air platform outside the sleeping room that is such a notable feature of traditional houses in Thailand itself.

Homes in the northern part of the present-day country were once probably similar to these, since winters there a thousand years ago, when the Thais began to drift down, were as cold as in China. Deforestation, rapidly increasing as more and more settlers arrived, led to warmer weather for much of the year and homes changed accordingly, acquiring

PAGE 54 **Detail of an eave of a Thai house. The decorative feature on the roof is a *ngao*, commonly found at the end of bargeboards.**

OPPOSITE **A mural painting in Wat Rajapradit, Bangkok (1864), showing the Royal Palace in the foreground. The domestic architecture includes houses on stilts, house boats and Chinese shophouses such as those found in Singapore and Malaysia.**

ABOVE **Northern Thai houses are similar in their design to these Laotian houses on stilts in this 19th-century engraving.**

FOLLOWING PAGES **This late 19th-century photograph by Robert Lenz captures a variety of wooden floating houses on the banks of the Chao Phraya River. This is the scene described by Joseph Conrad when he arrived in 1888 to take over his first command of a sailing ship.**

symbolises a pair of horns, citing the fact that in ancient times buffalo horns were often placed on roof-tops to show the wealth of the family. A number of studies are currently being made on the subject, but thus far the answer remains a matter of conjecture.

On the simplest houses, especially those made of bamboo, the *kalae* are nothing more than rather crude extensions, possibly serving a functional purpose by simplifying construction and further strengthening the roof. On a house belonging to a more prosperous family, however, they are often separate pieces beautifully carved in a shape that does indeed suggest feathers or perhaps flickering flames and that provides a decorative effect not unlike the curved finials at either end of Thai temple roofs. *Kalae* are also found on houses of some of the hill tribes who live in the northern mountains, as well as those of the Thai Lü people in southern China and Laos. They are rarely seen on houses in central and southern Thailand.

The classic northern house, rectangular in shape, is raised a considerable distance off the ground on sturdy round posts, and oriented north and south to expose it to the prevailing winds. Wood is used throughout and the walls, doors, windows and gable ends are made as separate units, an early form of prefabrication that was being practised in Thailand centuries before its advantages were recognised by Western architects. Using joints of wood held in place by wooden pegs—never nails in the older houses—the components are then hung on the pillars, the walls slanting outward from the floor to the lower edge of the roof, which is either

characteristics of the style now known as Lanna Thai. Stoves, used for cooking rather than for heating, were moved outside the sleeping quarters into a separate kitchen, often some distance away, and there were more and larger windows. As ventilation became an important consideration, the elevation of the house from the ground increased, creating a convenient open space below which could be used to keep domestic animals or for such activities as cloth-weaving and woodcarving.

The best-known northern-style dwelling today is the one popularly called a *kalae* house, the name being derived from a prominent V-shaped design formed by extending the roof supports beyond the ridge-pole on both ends of the structure. *Kalae* has been variously translated as 'glancing crows' and 'glancing pigeons', and some authorities believe one of its non-structural purposes may have been to discourage crows and other large birds from lighting on the roof. Others think the feature tiled, wood-shingled or thatched according to the fortunes of the owner. The outward-leaning walls are one of the marks that distinguish the northern house from that of the central plains, in which both the pillars and walls incline slightly inward toward the top, adding to its graceful suggestion of height.

Because teak was the most abundant building material in the northern hills, it was the wood favoured for construction of the better houses both in the north and in the central region. The pillars supporting the house, however, were traditionally of stronger wood, usually a pair of each variety. Certain woods were taboo, however, because their names in Thai had inauspicious associations. One, for instance, sounded like the word for 'corpse', while another, the *yon* tree, was never used because it was believed that it harboured spirits who might bring trouble to the residents. As we shall see later, similar beliefs come into play in the selection of plants for a Thai garden.

At the foot of the stairs leading to the upper platform, a trough of water is placed for washing the feet, since no shoes are worn above—a custom that has given rise to a northern saying that a wet lower step is a happy sign since it suggests the family is honoured by many visitors. Hospitable households in the region also often place an earthenware jar of cool water just outside the gate for the benefit of thirsty strangers who might pass by.

The smallest house consists of a covered but otherwise open verandah, slightly raised above the level of the upper platform, and behind it a large room that serves as the family sleeping quarters. Windows in the sleeping room are often small, perhaps a

legacy of the distant past, though it is likely to be cool thanks to the high roof and absence of a ceiling. The kitchen is separate, either a small room or a covered area on the platform. In large families, this basic plan may be elaborated so that two or more rooms, each an individual structure, are built on the platform. Eating and other family activities take place on the verandah, which also serves as a sleeping place for younger male members and male guests.

Aside from the *kalae* and the outward leaning walls, the classic northern-style house has another feature that distinguishes it from houses of central Thailand. The inner room, where the owner and his wife sleep, is believed to contain not only the ancestral spirits but also the virility and fertility of the couple who lives there. Above the doors leading to it are placed carved wooden lintels known as *ham yon*, which in the old language of the north can be translated as 'magic testicles', and these both preserve the strength of the family and protect it from outside evils.

A Chiang Mai scholar by the name of Kraisri Nimmanahaeminda, who donated his family home as an example of northern architecture to the Siam Society in Bangkok, has made a detailed study of the *ham yon*, rapidly becoming rare as Western-style houses replace traditional ones. Among other things, he discovered that the size of the lintels were determined by the length of the owner's foot, with a small one being three times the length and a large one four times as long. The designs, of uncertain symbolic intent, are at once decorative and highly varied—often stylised flowers, geometric designs or cloud-like patterns. Before the carver set about

ABOVE **Detail of a mural painting (late 19th century) in Wat Buak Krok Luang in Chiang Mai, showing couples inside a northern Thai house.**

his task, Mr Kraisri found, a ceremony was held in which the house owner offered food, flowers and candles to the magic power, inviting it to enter the lintel and assume the role of protector of the house. In his study he commented further:

"As the house ages, the ham yon... become more powerful. Often when an old house is sold, the new owner, before he moves in or dismantles it, will beat the ham yon mercilessly in order to destroy the magic accumulated in them under the old owner for it might bode ill for him. This beating of the lintel or 'testicles' is actually a symbolic 'castration'."

Mr Kraisri also offers two theories collected from the Thai Yuan, as northern Thais are sometimes known, to explain the peculiar shape of their houses. According to one, "the house is designed to resemble a huge buffalo planted firmly on its pillar-like legs, the body sloping out to massive shoulders supporting the head from which the horns rise. The *ham yon*, above the entrance to the private inner chamber, symbolise the genitals of the beast—the source of its power". The other is more fanciful and also more ominous; it holds that the outward-slanting walls and peaked roof of the house approximates the shape of a Burmese coffin and that the Thai Yuan were compelled to live in such inauspicious structures when the Burmese conquered them in the mid-16th century as a way of destroying them spiritually.

About 80 per cent of the components in both northern and central houses are prefabricated. There have been various speculations on the reasons for this eminently practical development. One claims that it arose in the workshops of master builders, which also served as schools; since the skills of carpentry were verbal, passed down from generation to generation through apprenticeship, it was more convenient to teach those skills applying to each part of a house in a single place where the various tools were readily available. Moreover, it was economical. When several house orders came in, the sections could be produced by a sort of assembly-line process, with the gable specialists working in one area, those who made walls in another, and so on.

It is also believed that the vogue for panelling walls—a distinctive feature of classic Thai style—was born in the workshops. According to one theory, these first appeared on houses built for the carpenters themselves as a thrifty way to use leftover wood. Sometimes relatively small pieces were fitted together with narrower bands to hold them in place, sometimes larger ones, both creating pleasing patterns on the otherwise plain walls. When prospective customers saw this innovation at the workshop, they were inspired to have it applied to the houses they ordered. Precisely when the practice became widespread is uncertain, but it may have been relatively recent as no mention of it is found in accounts by foreign travellers to Ayutthaya towards the end of the 17th century.

Another reason for prefabrication was undoubtedly that it made moving house far simpler. People who settled on the banks of a river or canal, as the majority of Thais did in the past, were regularly plagued by erosion or floods which necessitated a move to a new location. Often, too, whole communities were shifted—or decided to shift themselves—for one reason or another, such as war or the availability of better farming land. Thanks to the method of construction, the greater part of a house could be taken down from its framework, stacked neatly on barges or buffalo carts and transported to its new location.

Finally, prefabrication greatly speeded up building, as Western architects have discovered in the present century. This was a matter of particular importance in crowded urban areas like 17th-century Ayutthaya, which had a population of more than a million, and also in early Bangkok. Fire was a regular menace in such cities of wood and bamboo houses, and large neighbourhoods were often destroyed in a single conflagration. In 1687, Simon de la Loubère was in Ayutthaya on a mission when some 300 houses went up in flame; they were rebuilt within two days on the same location.

In the far south, a very different kind of traditional house developed, also influenced by climatic conditions. It consisted of a single unit, a long hall-like affair rather than a cluster of rooms, and there was usually no verandah. Windows had flap-like shutters held open with poles outside and closed during monsoon storms. The pillars supporting the house, rarely as high as those elsewhere in Thailand because of high winds, were often set inside large stones in which holes were drilled, thus giving the structure more strength in the sandy, often wet soil. Some prefabrication was practised with houses made of bamboo, for which the walls were made separately but not to the extent that it was elsewhere in the country. Smaller houses, nevertheless, could be easily moved by the simple expedient of placing

poles under them and lifting the whole structure, posts and all, off its stone supports.

The Thai house, usually regarded as the ultimate in classic styles, is the kind found throughout the central plains where the Thais achieved their greatest power and sense of cultural identity. Raised on round posts or floating in a river or canal, it has steep roofs with wide decorative bargeboards that rise to a sharp peak in the middle and curve gracefully upward at either end in a decorative feature known in Thai as *ngao*, which was developed from Khmer art during the Sukhothai period and which appears in many forms on religious buildings and palaces, all more elaborate than the version on the domestic house. Leaning slightly inward, possibly to increase the slope of the roof, the panelled walls seem to be straining towards the sky, suggesting in a suitably modest way the more substantial glory of Thai temples. Door thresholds are raised, making the prefabricated walls stronger, and some of the better houses have carved panels below the windows on the outside. Ideally adapted to the climate and to the cultural requirements of its

ABOVE *(left)* **Interior of a Thai house. Note the characteristic panelled walls, bare of any decoration except for some family pictures;** *(right)* **A verandah, with triangular cushions for relaxing. In Thailand, most social activities traditionally take place in open areas like this.**

residents, it is also a model of elegant lightness and, as increasing numbers of people are rediscovering, a beautiful creation that meets many modern needs as well as those of the past.

The exact evolution of the central Thai house remains something of a mystery, thanks to the lack of reliable research materials. In Sukhothai, the first Thai capital, both palaces and ordinary homes were constructed of perishable materials—probably bamboo, in the case of the latter—and no trace of either has survived. The same is true for most of Ayutthaya's 400-year history, when even though the kings adopted the Khmer concept of divine rule they continued for centuries to build their own palaces out of wood, reserving stones and masonry for religious structures. It was not until towards the end of the 17th century, in the reign of King Narai, that the first enduring royal buildings were put up, probably through the influence of Europeans who came at that time.

It is likely, however, that certain features of the central house appeared quite early in even the simplest bamboo-and-thatch version. High elevation from the ground was a practical necessity in a flat region subject to annual inundation, just as an open platform and a general sense of airiness was a logical answer to a hot, humid climate and the desire to spend as much time as possible outside the sleeping quarters. The steep roof with its long overhangs helped protect the inner room from the heavy rains that came regularly for three or four months out of the year. Moves were frequent among the peasant population in those days, so prefabrication offered both convenience and

economy. Finally, according to Thai custom, a son went to live with his wife's family after marriage—a practice that not only provided an extra worker for the family fields but also eliminated the conflicts between daughter and mother-in-law—and this led naturally to the so-called 'cluster house' in which several rooms share the same platform.

We do not know, however, just when the wooden central house acquired the distinctive appearance by which it is recognised today. De la Loubère, whose *Historical Relation of the Kingdom of Siam* is generally regarded as the best source of information on life in Ayutthaya at the peak of its prosperity, had this to say on the houses of the late 17th century:

OPPOSITE AND PAGE 67 **A range of Thai rooftops, both thatched and tiled. Note the various decorative features.**

ABOVE **A northern Thai house.**

ABOVE **A 17th-century engraving entitled 'A House of a Siamese', from Simon de la Loubère's account of his visit to Ayutthaya.**

"If the Siamese are plain in their habits, they are not less so in their homes, in their furniture, and in their food: rich in general poverty because they know how to content themselves with a little. Their houses are small, but surrounded with pretty large grounds. Hurdles of cleft bamboo, oftentimes not close compacted, do make the floors, walls, and roofs thereof. The piles, on which they are erected to avoid the inundation, are bamboos as thick as one's leg, and about 13 feet above the ground, by reason that the waters do sometimes rise as much as that. There is never more than four or six, on which they do lay other bamboos instead of beams. The stairs are a ladder of bamboo, which hangs on the outside like the ladder of a windmill."

De la Loubère also noted that high court officials lived in wooden houses, which they were careful to make "less exalted than the palaces [of the King]" and scotches the report that "no person may be higher in his own house than the King of Siam when he passes through the street mounted on his elephant"—an impossibility, he points out, considering the fact that the houses were erected on such high poles.

Nowhere in this detailed commentary, it will be noted, is there any mention of ornamentation, in particular of the wide curving bargeboards and panelled walls that are now such prominent features of the classic house. On the other hand, and in apparent contradiction, de la Loubère's work does include an engraving labelled 'A House of a Siamese' which though it has walls apparently made of woven bamboo is also adorned by roof decorations strikingly similar to those seen on

temples, not only on the eaves but also at either end of the roof. Whether this rendering is realistic or whether the artist embellished his sketches (as those who depicted the Thais themselves certainly did) must remain unknown; in support of the latter, however, is the fact that no such domestic Thai house appears in any mural painting of a slightly later period.

Only 75 years after de la Loubère's book appeared, Ayutthaya fell to the Burmese. Virtually the entire city was destroyed by fire, especially the bamboo and wooden structures that had housed the great majority of its population, leaving almost as much mystery surrounding their precise architecture as that which shrouds the ordinary homes of Sukhothai. Some authorities believe that the house we know today developed only at the very end of Ayutthaya and possibly not until the Bangkok period, which began in 1782. If so, then the development must have been remarkably fast for the structures can be seen in numerous murals painted in the early 19th century with all their classic features on display, looking very much like a well-established part of the landscape.

Various kinds of houses appear in these paintings, as they still do in many parts of rural Thailand. The smallest is a single unit with bedroom, kitchen, verandah and open platform, all of course elevated on posts. More common are the cluster houses, where as many as five bedrooms are arranged around the central platform, with the owner's room always occupying the most important place. Along the banks of rivers and canals, the structure may serve as both house and shop, with

the bedroom and kitchen in the rear and the open front used to display merchandise; a single piece of some light material, such as thatch, covers the front at night and is opened during business hours. Finally, there are the floating houses that attracted so much comment from early European visitors. These, too, are twin houses in which the family lives in the rear and trades in the one facing the water. Architecturally, they are the same as the others except that the planks of the floor are not as tightly fitted to allow for more movement as the stream rises and falls.

Simple as it may appear to an outsider, the Thai house embodies a complex accretion of symbols and beliefs covering almost every aspect of its construction and arrangement of living space. Before building commences, the future resident must consult an astrologer to determine the most suitable month. This will usually be January, March, April, August, November or December, though it may vary in particular cases. Once the month has been settled, further calculations are required to determine the proper day and time to begin placing the pillars in the ground. Traditionally, the best days for the initial post raising are Thursday, Friday and Saturday.

Alignment of the house on the plot of ground is equally important. S. J. Tambiah, an anthropologist who worked in Thailand, made this observation on the points of the compass in a north-east village, but they apply also in the north and central region:

"East is auspicious, represents life, is sacred … and is the direction of the rising sun. East is also, when one faces north, the direction of the right hand and represents male sex. West is inauspicious, represents death, impurity, and the setting sun. It also represents the left hand and the female sex. North is auspicious and is associated with the elephant, an auspicious animal because of its size, natural strength and its associations with royalty and Buddhist mythology. South is of neutral value."

Based on these values, according to his study: "Ideally a person entering the house would face the north and the entrance platform is at the southern end and the sleeping room at the northern end. The directions can be reversed. Never must the sleeping room be placed in the west. The kitchen and the washing place are also always on the western side of the house." In some cases, nature interferes with these arrangements, particularly when the house is on a waterway as was frequently the case in the past. Here, however, tradition is accommodating—water is believed to be auspicious enough to counteract any taboo, even a westerly orientation.

The size of the house determines the number of posts, but however many are used there must be an odd number of spaces between them, generally either three or five (just as there must also be an odd number of steps on the ladder or stair leading to the platform). Thus:

(1) ○ (2) ○ (3) ○ (4) ○ (5) ○
But never:
(1) ○ (2) ○ (3) ○ (4) ○

The posts are carefully selected for strength and smoothness and often auspicious names like king, diamond and happiness are inscribed on them. In central Thailand, the two most important posts are called *saaw eg* (first or primary post) and *saaw*

ABOVE **A guardian spirit house in the form of a typical cluster-style dwelling. Floral offerings are placed in front of the open verandah.**
OPPOSITE *(top)* **The jackfruit, or *kha-nun*, tree;** *(middle)* **The star gooseberry (*Phyllanthus acidus*) is traditionally planted near the gate of a house;** *(bottom)* **The intensely fragrant *Michelia champaca alba*, popular in many traditional gardens.**

khwan (post containing the spiritual essence). Usually the *saaw eg* will be part of the support for the east side of the main bedroom, across from the *saaw khwan*. On the day these two are placed in the ground—chosen by the builder on the basis of their perfection—a ceremony is performed to ask the spirit guarding the land for permission, with offerings of such delicacies as betel-nut, young coconut, boiled eggs, bananas and Thai desserts, all placed beside the hole. Later, a special little house, also raised on a pole, will be put somewhere on the property to serve as a spiritual abode and supplied with regular provisions and burning incense sticks. Usually this will be a miniature of the classic Thai house, though wealthier families may choose an ornate, multi-coloured affair that resembles a temple building.

Before the first and second posts are raised, they are decorated beforehand with young banana shrubs, stalks of sugar cane and lengths of sacred coloured cloth, and gold leaf is applied to the top of each. In some places, a piece of clothing belonging to the male of the household is tied to the first post and one belonging to his wife to the second. When these items are removed during construction, the plants often become a part of the garden. The men who carry the posts to the site and place them in the holes are chosen for having auspicious-sounding names, or at least given them for the duration of the ceremony; among the popular ones are *Phet* (diamond), *Thong Kham* (pure gold) and *Ngoen* (silver).

The arrangement of the various areas in the house is also a matter of tradition. The highest section is the main bedroom, generally about 40 centimetres above the verandah, which in turn is some 40 centimetres above the open platform. Doors and windows must always open inwards. The shelf or altar holding the family Buddha images faces east. The kitchen, being a place of no spiritual significance, is on the west. The washing area is on the lowest level. Toilets, when they exist, are usually in a separate structure elsewhere in the compound, though chamber pots are still widely used in many rural areas.

The date for moving in calls for further astrological calculations and may or may not coincide with the owner's wishes or even actual completion of the house. Monks are always invited in the morning to receive food, thus bringing merit to the owner and assuring his happiness, and a senior priest will ritually bless each of the main rooms.

The exterior simplicity of the traditional Thai house—besides the curving bargeboards, the only decoration usually found is the piece of carved wood under the windows and perhaps some more carving on the main door frame—is reflected in its furnishings. Since family activities customarily take place on the floor, there is always an ample supply of woven reed mats for sleeping or sitting. More prosperous families may have low beds and tables with curved legs in Chinese style and there may also be a low dressing table, used at floor level. The bedroom also generally contains a chest or cupboard to store clothes and other possessions. Water for the bathroom and kitchen is kept in large jars, sometimes glazed and decorated with dragons or other motifs. The kitchen contains a charcoal stove and a screened cabinet for dishes and foodstuffs.

Some colour and greenery are provided by pot plants on the open platform, selected for fragrance, beauty and names that in Thai suggest good fortune. Jasmine is a perennial favourite in the first category and crotons and caladiums are prominent among the last. There is also a large category of plants known by Thais as *wahn*, or lucky, each with its own auspicious-sounding name, and several pots of these can be found on nearly every platform.

The garden surrounding the house is mainly utilitarian, though traditional belief may also play a role. If there is a star gooseberry (*ma-yom* in Thai), it will be planted in front of the house since *yom* means 'admiration' and will thus attract people to the owners. Similarly, a jackfruit (*kha-nun*) will be grown behind since *nun* suggests the idea of support. Somewhere, there will be an area for the herbs and spices essential to any Thai kitchen: basil and mint, chilli peppers and lemon grass, ginger and coriander. Coconut palms are common, as are such fruit trees as mango, tamarind, guava and rose apple. An old-fashioned garden will also contain a number of plants whose roots, leaves or flowers can be used for medicinal purposes. Not surprisingly, there are certain plants which tradition says must not be grown. Frangipani (*plumeria*) is taboo because its Thai name, *lan-tom*, sounds like *ra-tom*, which means 'sorrow'. The Bodhi tree is forbidden because of its association with Buddhism and most other members of the Ficus family because they are believed to harbour spirits. *Bombax malabaricum*, a native tree whose orange-red flowers are used in soup by northerners, is frowned upon for two compelling reasons: its soft wood is popular with coffin-makers and also in depictions of Buddhist hell unfaithful husbands and wives are shown climbing its trunk with a tiger in hot pursuit.

At the time P. A. Thompson came to Thailand, houses of the kind described here were as characteristic of the landscape as the fabulous Buddhist temples. Within a generation they had almost vanished from Bangkok and were becoming increasingly rare in the countryside as new building materials and new lifestyles found favour. Only in relatively recent years has there been a renewed appreciation of their beauty and practicality, and it has come, paradoxically, from the same affluent group which was the first to abandon the old style.

THIS PAGE **Floating houses in Uthai Thani Province.**

OPPOSITE **Floating structures along the Chao Phraya River at Uthai Thani.**

Floating Houses

In the past, most communities were located on rivers or canals and many of the houses were literally in the water, either floating or anchored on posts. As these pictures show, the old custom is still followed in many parts of the country. Wood was the traditional building material in old Thailand, employed on both Thai-style houses and those that later displayed Western influences. Roofs were generally tiled or thatched, steeply sloped and had broad eaves to protect the interior from sunlight and rain. Elaborate fretwork adorned many buildings of the late 19th and early 20th centuries.

RIGHT **Side view of the Prince of Lampang's residence, with a horse cart of a type still used in the northern city of Lampang.**
BOTTOM **Detail of a mural painting in the Vihan Laikham at Wat Phra Singh in Chiang Mai. The roof decorations are similar to those on the Prince of Lampang's palace.**
OPPOSITE **Front view of the palace. Note the finials, or *chofahs*, at the top of the roofs. Though more commonly used on temples, they sometimes appeared on royal palaces.**

Palace of a Prince

The Prince of Lampang's palace, known as the Ho Kham or 'gilded hall', was built in the provincial capital of Lampang during the early Bangkok period. The original building was pulled down in the 1930s; the one shown here was reconstructed from old photographs at an outdoor museum called the Ancient City just outside Bangkok, where numerous classic buildings and careful reproductions from Thailand's past are displayed in a large area. The residence, in northern style, is made entirely of timber without nails and raised off the ground on large posts.

A King's Residence

This house dates from the latter part of the 18th century and once served as the residence of King Rama I before he came to the throne and founded the Chakri Dynasty. He donated the structure to Wat Rakhang Kositaram in Dhonburi to serve as a repository for sacred scriptures. After becoming king, he ordered extensive renovations, among them the carved doors and the mural paintings on the interior walls. The house consists of three units joined together, with a number of its architectural features altered when it was reconstructed in the temple compound. The murals were the work of Phra Acharn Nak, one of the few early artists whose names are known today, and depict kneeling Thai divinities as well as scenes from the *Ramakien* epic.

Baan Sao Nak

Baan Sao Nak, or 'the house of numerous pillars', stands in the northern city of Lampang and was home to Khunying Walai Leelanuch, principal of the Lampang Kallayanee School. Combining Lanna Thai and Burmese styles, it is believed to have been originally erected in 1896 by the past owner's grandparents who were of Burmese origin. It stands on 116 teak pillars, giving rise to its popular name.

Starting in 1964 and continuing all the way until 1974, extensive repairs were carried out on the house. Concrete plinths were added to the pillars to prevent further sinking of the large structure; the wooden floorboards of the porch were entirely replaced with tiles; and then the gutter, originally made from teak carved as a channel, was covered with galvanised iron.

In 1987, Khunying Walai decided to replace an old rice barn which has been a part of the compound with another built in traditional style and resting on 24 pillars. The barn was consecrated in an elaborate ceremony involving ancient northern rituals in March of 1988. Since the demise of Khunying Walai, the house has been a museum and is popular with both locals and tourists alike.

OPPOSITE **The rice barn, with its 24 pillars. Rice barns are a traditional feature of northern compounds.**

ABOVE **A view of the front of Baan Sao Nak, showing the entrance stairway.**

The Kamthieng House

The Kamthieng House stands in the Bangkok compound of the Siam Society, a scholarly organisation established in 1904, and serves today as an ethnological museum. Dating from the middle of the 19th century, the traditional northern-style house formerly stood on the east bank of the Ping River in Chiang Mai. It was donated to the Society in the 1960s by Khun Kraisri Nimmanahaeminda, a businessman and scholar from Chiang Mai, and named in honour of his grandmother, Nang Kamthieng Anusarasundara, who was born in the house. The structure contains a living area, a covered verandah, an open platform and a kitchen. Connected by a walkway is a teak rice granary which the Society also acquired in Chiang Mai. Various items used in daily life are displayed in the buildings.

OPPOSITE *(top)* The verandah, on which are displayed an elephant *howdah*, a rice container and a bamboo device for carrying water jars; *(bottom)* The kitchen of the Kamthieng House, with a collection of typical cooking pots, glutinous rice baskets and other kitchen utensils.

LEFT The rice granary, under which is a buffalo cart commonly used by farmers in the region.

Traditions Renewed

THIS PAGE **On a field in Anthong, workers make the components of a Thai house, nearly all of which are prefabricated and then assembled on the building site.**

OPPOSITE **Khun Reuycharoeng's home serves as a model for customers wishing to select details of construction and decoration.**

Khun S. Reuycharoeng in Angthong employs a large number of skilled craftsmen to produce traditional Thai houses. The business has been responsible for numerous homes in various parts of Thailand, particularly Bangkok. Several years ago, a team of builders was sent to Monte Carlo where they assembled a pavilion for a wealthy resident who had admired the structure on a visit to Thailand.

Thai Gardens

The gardens of most traditional Thai houses, in the past and to a large extent in the present, are limited to trees and shrubs with a practical use, either for food or medicine. Generally this means fruit trees, such as mango, banana, tamarind and rose apple, and assorted herbs used in Thai cooking, such as chilli peppers, basil and lemon grass.

In royal palaces and temples, however, decorative plants and more attention to overall design are common. The major influence in these landscapes is Chinese, as can been seen in such features as shrubs clipped into assorted shapes, a form of topiary art known in Thai as *mai dat*, artificial mountains and ponds or water jars planted with lotus and water lilies.

OPPOSITE **A *mai dat* garden in Wat Po, the Temple of the Reclining Buddha, Bangkok.**
THIS PAGE **The grounds of the Royal Palace in Bangkok feature clipped trees, or *mai dat*, and a Chinese-style garden.**
FOLLOWING PAGES **The lush gardens of the Prasat Museum, Bangkok.**

Traditions Adapted

Once an endangered form of architecture, the traditional Thai-style house is now enjoying a revival as many homeowners seek to adapt its simple, classic beauty for more contemporary styles of living.

PAGE 90 **The drawing room of the Jim Thompson house opens out to a terrace paved with 17th-century bricks from Ayutthaya and leads to a pavilion on a canal.**
ABOVE **The entrance courtyard of the Jim Thompson house, with its distinctive Thai roofs.**

In a village near the old capital of Ayutthaya, dozens of doors, panelled walls, gables and other components of the classic Thai house are neatly stacked under a simple shelter overlooking a rice field. Fifty years ago, perhaps less, all would have been destined for one of the farming families in the area and take their place in a traditional village setting. Today, most will end up in Bangkok gardens, overlooked by towering office blocks and condominiums. Some may even go much further—to Hawaii, perhaps, or to the south of France—to shelter strangers who have never heard of the village where they were created but whose imaginations have been fired by a glimpse of Thailand's traditional domestic architecture being used as a backdrop for modern living.

Some date this development from the spring of 1959 when Jim Thompson, the American who revived the Thai silk industry, moved into a Thai-style house on a Bangkok *klong*. It was not the only such structure to be seen in the capital at the time nor the largest; several members of the royal family could point to impressive ancestral homes in their spacious compounds and the distinctive peaked roofs were then still fairly common in older neighbourhoods, though their owners often regarded them as old-fashioned and uncomfortable. What made the Thompson house different from most of these was the fact that he had adapted the classic concepts to the needs of a contemporary lifestyle and shown in a dramatic way that they remained practical as well as beautiful.

"Jim Thompson's Thai House" appears on most tourist itineraries today and hundreds of visitors come weekly to admire his extensive collection of Asian art displayed in it. The majority are equally impressed by the house itself, rising with serene elegance out of a lush garden, though few perhaps understand the numerous ways—some subtle, some drastic—in which Thompson modified the traditional architecture to achieve his goal. Residents, Thai as well as foreign, inspected his innovations more carefully and many were inspired to emulate them, not only in Bangkok but also in other parts of the country. It may be overstating the case to say that Jim Thompson performed the same service for Thai domestic houses that he did for the country's silk, but there can be little doubt that he was responsible in large part for the subsequent boom in such structures, prompting buyers to seek out surviving houses and bringing a flood of orders to carpenters skilled in the old crafts like those in Ayutthaya.

As more than a few have discovered, the transformation involves more than merely assembling the components thus acquired. The classic house was well suited to the simple needs of rural life in the past. It was open and airy, had space below for the family's domestic animals and, with its arrangement of separate rooms around a platform, could accommodate various members in a way that reflected their status. Most of these advantages become either irrelevant or downright inconvenient in an urban setting. Privacy, an alien concept to Thai villagers, assumed a far greater importance when strangers as well as friendly neighbours might be peering in. Conveniences like air-conditioning and modern bathrooms, essential to sophisticated city dwellers, had to somehow be installed. Moreover, many wanted easier passage from room to room than the traditional arrangement allowed.

The problem, essentially, was how to adapt a traditional house to these requirements without destroying its architectural distinction. Some unhappy hybrids have resulted, blending various styles incongruously or failing to respect the proportions that contribute so importantly to the elegance of the true Thai house. But as the following pages show, a number have been notably successful, even when apparently violating basic tenets. Jim Thompson, for example, linked the assorted houses by connecting passageways, insisted on an enclosed stairwell and reversed the walls of the drawing room so that the carvings under the windows faced inward. Others have incorporated swimming pools, jacuzzis, steam baths and an assortment of other decidedly non-traditional amenities. Yet in doing so, they have nonetheless managed to preserve the basic Thai flavour so that the houses retain their artistic integrity while also offering the comforts their owners desire.

BELOW **Architectural plan of the Jim Thompson house, as seen from the front. The large central structure contains the spacious drawing room and is flanked by smaller houses on either side.**

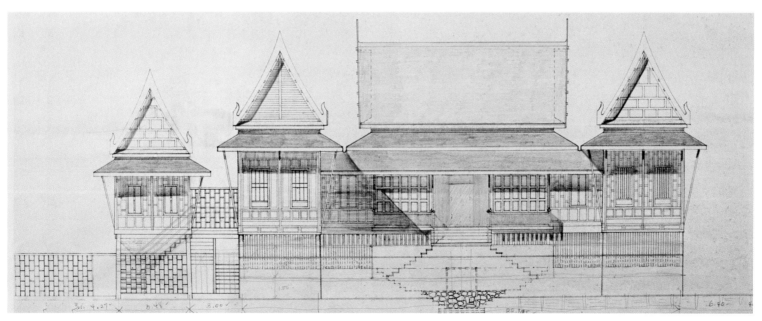

BOTTOM **Carved teakwood doors from Ayutthaya, probably 18th century, with a design of climbing plants and birds.**
OPPOSITE **The terrace off the drawing room of the Jim Thompson house is paved with 17th-century bricks from Ayutthaya. To its right is the dining room. Facing the terrace but hidden by lush shrubbery is a canal that runs through central Bangkok.**

The House on the Klong

Four old central Thai houses and part of a fifth were used in the construction of Jim Thompson's famous house, located on a canal in the centre of modern Bangkok. The largest and oldest, dating from around 1800, forms the drawing room and came from a silk-weaving village across the canal, as did the one housing the kitchen. The rest were brought downriver from a village near the old capital of Ayutthaya. Thompson enclosed the staircase in a marble-floored hallway, joined the rooms with connecting roofs, added modern baths and reversed the walls of the drawing room so that the carvings below the windows faced inward.

Work was started on the house in September of 1958 and it was completed in April of the following year. Since Thompson's disappearance in 1967, it has been maintained as a museum under royal patronage and is visited by some 500 people a day.

ABOVE The dining room. The porcelain on the dining table is Annamese and was made in the Ming Dynasty. The chandelier is from a 19th-century Bangkok palace.

OPPOSITE *(bottom left)* **A selection of blue-and-white porcelain from Jim Thompson's extensive collection, mostly dating from the Ming period;** *(bottom right)* **Specimens of Bencharong porcelain, made in China with Thai designs, grace a shelf in Jim Thompson's house.**

ABOVE **The drawing room. The large coffee table that dominates the room was once a bed. A Burmese Buddha image sits on a table next to the window, while to the left of the teak column is a gold-and-black lacquered manuscript cabinet.**

RIGHT The master bedroom, with a carved teak bed, Thai silk cushions and assorted antiques. The door to the right leads to a screened verandah.

FAR RIGHT *(top)* Painted wood detail of mythological Thai figures on a scripture cabinet; *(middle)* Doors and display windows from an old Chinese pawnshop form a wall leading from the drawing room to the bedroom wing; *(bottom)* A limestone Buddha image of the Dvaravati period (6th to 10th century) takes pride of place in an alcove in the study.

Elegant Entertaining

The late Mrs Connie Mangskau, one of Bangkok's leading dealers in decorative arts, was inspired to build a Thai-style house for entertaining by her friend Jim Thompson. A number of old houses, mostly acquired near Ayutthaya, were used on three sides of a raised platform overlooking a garden. After her death, the house was sold and moved to a new location just outside Bangkok, though with the spacious central room somewhat reduced in size.

OPPOSITE **The living room, which occupies one side of the upper terrace. Among the items on display are a large Thai bed, a pair of Burmese priests in lacquered wood, an ivory betel-nut set and a tapestry-size Thai painting on cloth.** ABOVE **A view from the lawn shows the large terrace which the owner used for entertaining.**

Vintage Structures

The structures that comprise the house of the late Tula Bunnag and his wife Chan Cham were mostly old ones found near Ayutthaya, brought to Bangkok and assembled in 1965. Four are arranged around a central platform and a fifth was added later at a lower level for a son's family. The entrance stair has been left uncovered in the traditional style.

A gifted woodcarver, Tula Bunnag provided many decorative features for the houses himself, among them window carvings that depict the animal zodiacs of the years in which he and his wife were born. His fine mother-of-pearl inlay work, which can also be seen on many objects displayed in the houses, complement the traditional furniture that furnish the place.

OPPOSITE A view of the interior of Tula Bunnag's house. Among the furnishings are a carved wooden cabinet, a fine dressing table and a gold-and-black lacquer chest for storing manuscript books. LEFT The Buddha Room, where homage is paid each day to the various images. The room is located off the central platform of the house. ABOVE Buddha images belonging to the family.

ABOVE **View of the Bunnag house from the garden.**

RIGHT **This is the house that Tula Bunnag built for one of his sons. It stands adjacent to the main dwelling. The woodcarvings under the windows were also done by him.**

OPPOSITE *(top)* **The living room and part of the covered verandah of the son's house. The Thai painting above the 19th-century cane chair is on wood;** *(bottom)* **The living room of the main house. In the corner is a carved wooden shrine for displaying religious objects; the scripture cabinet on the right is decorated with gold and black lacquer. The small plaque of black lacquer inlaid with mother-of-pearl was made by Tula Bunnag.**

Traditional—With a Modern Flair

The Bangkok home of Patsri and Jean-Michael Beurdeley gives the impression of being an old northern-style house that has been moved to the capital. Actually, it was entirely new when it was built several decades ago. Most of the woodcarvings used in its decorations, though, are antiques collected in the north of Thailand.

A small swimming pool has been incorporated into the design, around which are four separate units containing a living room, a dining room, a master bedroom and guest rooms. The kitchen is located downstairs. Francois Catroux, a Paris-based decorator, designed the living room using a parquet floor with a sunken area for displaying plants. The panelled walls of the dining room were the creation of a Bangkok antique dealer, Somkid Thanapoomikul.

OPPOSITE **Painted doors and panels from northern Thailand enliven the guest bedroom. The paintings depict guardian figures surrounded by Thai motifs.**
BELOW **A painted cabinet, on which is displayed a fragment of a Khmer stone head.**

OPPOSITE *(top)* The low couch was made from pieces of old carved wood. Forming a dramatic backdrop are panels from a northern temple. A painted cabinet for storing manuscript books stands against the left wall; *(bottom left)* An elephant *howdah*; *(bottom right)* A carved lintel showing monkey gods. LEFT The dining room with a Chinese scroll and covered brass bowls in the shape of sprouting coconuts. The wall panels are new and were supplied by a Bangkok art dealer. FOLLOWING PAGES The living room features a sunken area for potted plants, low cushions covered in Thai cotton, a Thai table and two northern manuscript cabinets. All these have been artfully put together to create an inviting space.

On the Chao Phraya

This group of Thai-style structures on the Chao Phraya River was originally built by the late Achille Clarac, former French ambassador to Thailand, and his son, Henri. A thick riverside stand of nipa palms screens the front of the property, which still preserves a rural atmosphere though it can be reached by boat from the centre of Bangkok in a short time. The main house consists of a living room, dining room and two bedrooms around an open platform. A separate guest pavilion overlooks a pool in an extensive garden planted with a variety of tropical shrubs, trees and palms. A complex hydraulic system helps protect the compound from flooding during high river tides that come at the end of the rainy season.

OPPOSITE *(far left)* **This small Thai-style structure not only conceals one of the many pumps used in flood control, it serves as a decorative feature in the garden;** *(top)* **A wooden walkway leads from a landing on the river—through a dense growth of nipa palms, the fronds of which are commonly used in the countryside for thatching—to the compound;** *(bottom)* **An entrance pavilion stands at the top of the central platform around which the rooms of the main house are arranged.**

LEFT **Paved with laterite blocks, the area under the house opens directly onto the garden and provides a cool sitting area. Old Thai jars are planted with water lilies and lotus.**

FOLLOWING PAGES **The garden of the Clarac compound is densely planted with palms, heliconias and other tropical specimens. On the right is the guest pavilion, adorned by an old pediment.**

ABOVE *(left)* **A view of the guest wing, which also contains the kitchen and servants' quarters;** *(right)* **The furniture in the living room and elsewhere in the house was made by Bangkok designer Khun Chantaka Puranananda.** OPPOSITE **The master bedroom is decorated with cushions and a bedspread in Thai silk.**

Traditions Revamped

The four Thai-style houses and garden pavilion that comprise this grouping—built in the same Bangkok compound with a Western-style family home—were constructed by Khun S. Reuycharoeng's company in Angthong (see pages 84–85). Carpenters skilled in the old crafts lived on the site during assembly of the prefabricated sections.

On one part of the main house containing the dining room, a base of laterite stone and modern glass windows was employed to allow more light into the interior and also to facilitate air-conditioning. Among the other modern facilities is a marble bathroom complete with a jacuzzi and steamroom; here translucent glass bricks allow natural light to come through.

In addition to the two main houses that are joined by a wooden deck, a separate structure consisting of two other houses contains the guest rooms, kitchen and servants' quarters.

THIS PAGE (above) **The spirit house;**
(right top) **The dining room where
a laterite base has been added
to allow the installation of
windows that not only provide
a view of the garden but allow
for air-conditioning comfort;**
(right bottom) **A view of the
bathroom with jacuzzi.**
OPPOSITE **The rear of the house,
with a deck overlooking a small
but atmospheric lily pond.**

Thai-Western Compromise

The owner of the house shown on these pages wanted to live in a Western-style dwelling yet also enjoy the open elegance of Thailand's classic domestic architecture. The problem was solved by Alicia de Guzman, a Filipina architect who has worked in Bangkok for many years, through the use of Thai-style structures for entertainment areas, guest quarters and the kitchen, and connecting them with a modern house at the back by way of an open-sided lobby. A system of waterways and ponds surrounds the buildings, and privacy has been achieved through planting trees and stands of bamboo.

ABOVE **An inviting space has been created on this open platform. Note the broad teak planks that form the floor.**
RIGHT **These entrance steps lead to a traditional pavilion where guests are received.**
OPPOSITE **A view of the house and grounds.**

OPPOSITE *(top)* **A large painting framed in old wood overlooks the dining area. The cushions are covered with cotton made by northern hill tribes. Prehistoric pots stand on the shelf above the bench;** *(bottom)* **The area connecting various parts of the house is open and sparsely furnished, and cooled by an old ceiling fan. The reclining chairs are typical of the furniture that appeared in Thai homes with the rise of Western influences in the late 19th century.**

LEFT **The entrance to the main room in the Thai-style part of the house. Above the door is a large painting on wood. The matchstick blinds can be lowered during storms to protect the interior from wind and rain.**

ABOVE **The kitchen, in which an old Thai cabinet is used for storing glassware.**

Art Studio and Home

Having enjoyed a traditional Thai *sala* (open sided pavilion) in their garden for several years, Khun Venica's parents brought the units that comprised this Thai house down from Ayutthaya in 1961 and reassembled them on their Bangkok property. All were around 80 to 100 years old. Three units, connected by walkways, were arranged around a pond. For several years, the largest served as a studio for Khun Venica's graphic design company, while she and her husband lived in the other rooms.

LEFT **The studio of Khun Venica's design company.**
ABOVE **Verandah of the house that contains the living quarters.**

ABOVE **Verandah of the house.
Thai-style lighting fixtures
hang from the ceiling, while the
carved wooden screen on the
left is from India.**
BOTTOM *(left)* **The bathroom;**
(right) **The living room holds an
old dressing table in red lacquer.**

ABOVE **Another section of the verandah outside the art studio. A traditional Thai painting hangs on the rear wall above two old ship's lanterns displayed on a Thai table.**

RIGHT **View of the guest pavilion showing the elegant rooftop decoration that defines it as Chiang Mai.**

OPPOSITE **The courtyard of the house is paved with laterite blocks and softened with lush tropical planting. One of Theo Meier's paintings can be seen on the wall of the entrance area.**

The Theo Meier House

Theo Meier was a Swiss-born painter who spent much of his life in Bali, where his Gauguinesque work attracted wide interest among art collectors. He moved to Thailand in the 1960s at the invitation of Prince Sanidh Rangsit, an old friend, and settled with his Thai wife, Laiad, in Chiang Mai, where he built a remarkable house on the bank of the Ping River. Since Meier's death, his widow has continued to live in the house where they entertained a constant stream of admiring guests.

The main house consists of three bedrooms and a large verandah overlooking the river, where most of the social life took place. There is also a guesthouse composed of three rooms and a *sala* just inside the gate. Another pavilion was later added to the compound, adjacent to Meier's riverside studio.

RIGHT This pavilion overlooking the Ping River was added to the compound by Meier's wife. The painted columns and other sections came from a northern temple.

OPPOSITE *(top)* The riverside pavilion, showing columns painted with typical northern motifs in gold. Locally woven cotton is used on cushions and as a tablecloth. The triangular marks on the doors were placed there by the presiding priest during the ceremony to bless the pavilion; *(bottom)* Dining table on verandah of the main house. On the wall hangs one of Meier's paintings of Chiang Mai orchids.

OPPOSITE **Some examples of woodcarvings that can be found on the various houses in the compound of Theo Meier's home. Most of them are the work of contemporary Chiang Mai artisans.**

LEFT TOP **Part of the main house in its jungle-like setting of vine-hung trees and tall native bamboo.**

LEFT BOTTOM **Verandah of the main house looking towards the entrance. The footed red-lacquer tray is northern Thai, while the patterned cloths are Indonesian.**

ABOVE **General view of the house. Note the ornamentation on the rooftops. In the garden is an old northern ox cart.**
RIGHT **The landing on the river.**
OPPOSITE **A view of the guest house, which was once a rice barn, from the garden.**

Northern Holiday House

Located on the outskirts of a village on the Ping River, about 15 kilometres from Chiang Mai, this northern-style house was built by a Bangkok couple as a holiday retreat. It consists of a main dwelling, separate guest quarters and a pavilion, all on a raised platform overlooking the river. Both old and new elements were used in the construction.

OPPOSITE **An old woodcarving in the bedroom makes a dramatic headboard for the traditional Thai bed.**
ABOVE **The sitting room.**
BOTTOM *(left)* **A Javanese cut-out figure;** *(right)* **A northern water jar with dipper. Such jars are placed outside homes to provide refreshment for thirsty strangers.**

RIGHT TOP **The main house of the Suanduenchai family. The steps lead to the entrance platform. This house and others in the compound were acquired in the Chiang Mai area and moved to the site when the original family home was destroyed by fire some years ago.**

RIGHT BOTTOM **This area below the guest house is used for weaving cotton.**

OPPOSITE **A view of the guest house from the platform of the main dwelling. The jar on the right beside the entrance gate contains water used by guests to wash their feet when arriving. A papaya tree can be seen growing at the bottom of the stairs.**

Chiang Mai Rustic

The rustic Chiang Mai home of Somphan and Nongkran Suanduenchai, owners of the Indigo Restaurant and Gallery and collectors of northern Thai textiles, consists of four northern-style structures around 60 to 80 years old—the main house, a guest house, a rice barn and a kitchen and servants' quarters. Chiang Mai is the traditional centre of Thai handicrafts, ranging from woodcarving to lacquer, and the house contains many examples among its furnishings, such as hand-woven cloth, baskets and other items typical of a northern home that has been relatively untouched by Western influences.

RIGHT The dining area in the main house is located on the covered but otherwise open platform at the top of the entrance stairs. The lamp shades are fish traps found in most parts of Thailand, while the elephant plaque above the door came from a northern buffalo cart. An old Thai cabinet stands against the far wall inside the house.

OPPOSITE (both) Two of the three bedrooms in the house. The textiles are cotton and display traditional patterns. The carved dressing table in the bottom picture is of northern workmanship.

On the Beach

Hua Hin, on the Gulf of Thailand, became a popular resort in the 1920s when the southern railway line made it easily accessible to Bangkok. The King built a summer palace there and many members of the Thai aristocracy soon followed to spend the hot-season months. The holiday compound shown here consists of five separate Thai houses, some old and some new. They were erected in the late 1970s by Khun Chantaka Puranananda on land belonging to his family. The furnishings are from Pure Design, Khun Chantaka's interior decoration company in Bangkok.

OPPOSITE **The house as seen from the beach at high tide.**

THIS PAGE (both) **Views of the tiled terrace shaded by casuarina trees.**

Sri Deva Giri

Yvan van Outrive and Wongvipa Devahstin na Ayutthaya drew on both northern Thai and Balinese sources in creating this remarkable residence in the Mae Rim district of Chiang Mai. It has since been acquired by a new owner. Lanfaa Davahastin na Ayutthaya contributed ideas in the conceptional design for the project and Surasak Hutaseevee worked on the large garden of rare and exotic plants gathered widely from all over the tropics.

Dominating the property is a multi-roofed northern-style pavilion, richly adorned with an old carved temple gable and 18 red columns stenciled with traditional gold designs. Open on all sides and offering views of rice fields, this offers a dramatic place for entertaining. Other buildings, including a private sauna with an outdoor bathing area, reflect Balinese influences. Water is a prominent feature of the garden, from a serene lake to a waterfall spilling over large boulders brought to the site.

OPPOSITE **The open-sided northern-style pavilion roofed with handmade terracotta tiles. Note the old temple gable and red columns.**

BELOW **Stepping stones lead across a reflecting pool to one of the buildings in the compound.**

RIGHT TOP **This imposing entrance leads to the living quarters.**

RIGHT BOTTOM **Steps leading to the garden pavilion are flanked by stone elephants.**

OPPOSITE **The grand interior of the pavilion. An antique bell hangs on the far side, while silk-covered cushions provide colourful accents in the spacious seating area.**

RIGHT The library, with a
locally-made teak desk.
Ornamental Thai figurines
on the shelf add local flavour
to the ambience of the room.
OPPOSITE A cabinet decorated
with traditional designs, plush
carpet and a comfortable
northern-style lounging chair
makes a cosy corner in the
living room that looks out to
a lush, tropical garden.

Entertaining Thai Style

In villages, both entertainment and ordinary meals nearly always took place on the raised open-air platform that was a prominent feature of traditional houses. They were cooler than the darker, more confined structures surrounding it. Here guests and family members sat or reclined on floor mats around low tables while enjoying a selection of dishes brought from the kitchen, conveniently located nearby.

Outdoor entertaining is equally popular in adapted, contemporary Thai-style homes, especially when there is a luxuriant tropical garden to add to the visual pleasure. The interiors of such houses are also often transformed into comfortable living spaces, with atmospheric lighting, polished wood floors, antiques of various kinds and cushions covered in locally woven silks and cottons.

OPPOSITE **The living room of this Thai house has been adapted to contemporary living, with a huge antique coffee table that takes centrestage, vibrant pendant lamps and numerous cushions for comfort.**
BELOW **Views of the garden add to the appeal of this room in an adapted Thai house.**

151

Foreign Influences

Although the first Western influences on Thai architecture were felt in the Ayutthaya period, the process did not gain real momentum until the late 19th century when it transformed Bangkok's appearance.

Robert Hunter, an Englishman who arrived in Bangkok in 1824 and became the capital's most influential foreign resident for nearly 20 years, has two claims to fame: he discovered the famous Siamese twins one day while crossing the Chao Phraya River and he built the first brick house of European design in the city. While the twins left Thailand and went on to fame and fortune in the West, eventually ending their days in North Carolina, Hunter's house marked the beginning of an architectural revolution that would soon drastically transform the traditional capital founded by King Rama I in 1782.

The Chao Phraya was the main street of early Bangkok, overlooked by the splendid mile-square Grand Palace and numerous Buddhist monasteries. Most commoners were compelled to live in floating houses moored by the hundreds along the bank, a rule that irked some of the foreign community, among them American missionaries, European diplomats and traders like Hunter. At least one of the reasons for their discomfort was revealed in a memoir by F. A. Neale, another Englishman who served with the Royal Siamese Navy in the same period:

"Mr Hunter's floating house was double the size of any of the others, very neatly painted and well furnished, with a nice little verandah in front. The first night of my arrival I was dining there with all the English and Portuguese then assembled at Bangkok; we dined late, by candlelight, and after dinner, walking up and down the verandah chatting about many little affairs, and the latest news, etc, I got so absorbed in the theme of the conversation as literally to forget that I was still upon the water; and taking one step too much, found myself all of a sudden up to my neck in water,

with the tide running so strong, that I lost hold of one of the wooden pillars of the verandah; and though I am by no means a bad swimmer, I should inevitably have been drowned that night by being drawn right under the houses, if assistance had not come."

Perhaps there were other such mishaps in the course of convivial gatherings. Dr Dan Beach Bradley, one of the American missionaries, hinted darkly in his journal about Hunter's "reputation as a tippler"; and if so, that may have been why Hunter finally used his influence in royal circles to gain permission for Europeans to build on solid ground. He himself was the first to take advantage of the ruling and put up what Neale described as "a very fine large prominent house, opposite to which the British ensign proudly floated on feast days and high days". A contemporary engraving shows it to have been a spacious, two-storey affair with a verandah on the river, several solid-looking outbuildings which were probably servants' quarters as well as a landing stage.

The rest of the foreigners soon followed. The Portuguese, who were the first of the Europeans to establish relations with Thailand during the Ayutthaya period, had already been granted a choice site by King Rama II for a 'factory', or trading post. According to Neale, they originally planned "a splendid brick palace as a fit residence for their envoy at this illustrious court", but the ship bringing high-quality bricks as well as skilled masons from Goa was wrecked in a storm on the way. The first European legation to rise in the city, as a result, was "very indifferently constructed with bamboo, poles, lath and plaster, but it was an extensive house, cleanly white-washed, neatly furnished and suited in one of the pleasantest positions in Siam". Some American missionaries settled nearby, their houses and the consulate forming a square in which grew a shady old tamarind tree of impressive size. Wrote Neale:

"Under this tree Signor Marsinello de Rosa had constructed a few pretty garden seats and reared a few choice flowers. And on this spot of a morning, before the sun's rays had waxed too warm, and of an evening after the heat of day had passed, the consul and his sedate neighbours used to assemble and discuss the latest news of the day, or watch the gay scene the river presented, or turn to the more gloomy themes and moralise on life and its many uncertain tenures."

As the 19th century progressed, a substantial number of other Western-style buildings joined these on both banks of the river. British, French and American legations were established not far from the Portuguese, who gradually improved the building described by Neale and began turning it into the structure that still stands today. Dr Bradley's Baptist Mission—a different group from those who enjoyed philosophical discussions under the tamarind tree with the Portuguese consul—lived in several uncomfortable places before they finally received permission to build on a site across the Chao Phraya. "While we felt it right and suitable that we should have large and roomy dwellings", Dr Bradley wrote, a bit waspishly, "we did not then feel justified in seeking nearly as expensive a finish on them as we had observed on the London Missionary Society dwellings in Penang and Singapore". The style decided on was typical of most foreign dwellings of the period, a few of which survive in the neighbourhood:

"Ours were made of wood, two tall stories high, covered with the common tiles of the country. They had verandahs all around them, with plank floors, ... and the rooms were all ceiled with rough boards whitewashed. The doors and windows especially were a great improvement on all their predecessors, being many and large, with posts plumb, and not leaning together or within, after the then universal custom of Siam, and the upper part of the window shutters were made of a coarse kind of Venetian blinds."

Having been rescued from the inconveniences of floating houses, the Europeans discovered a new one on land—the lack of proper roads along which they could enjoy an evening stroll or a carriage ride. Once more they turned for assistance to the ruler, who by this time was the remarkable King Mongkut, or Rama IV. Already committed to modernising his kingdom—he put up the first Western buildings in the Grand Palace compound (one of them inspired by London's Big Ben) and hired an Englishwoman named Anna Leonowens to teach some of his children—the king was

BELOW **An old photograph of New Road, Bangkok's first real street, built in the mid-19th century.**

sympathetic to the complaint and initiated a road-building programme.

One of the thoroughfares that resulted was Charoen Krung, known to the foreign colony as New Road, which ran along the river just behind the legations all the way to the Chinese quarter. The latter was by then a densely populated area, thanks to a flood of Chinese immigrants, and solid buildings of brick and mortar were appearing there too, as well as across the river where many of the larger godowns were located. By the end of Mongkut's reign, Charoen Krung and the lanes leading off it were lined with shophouses, small hotels and various other establishments and was Bangkok's acknowledged centre of commerce and foreign architecture.

The transformation of the city increased rapidly under Mongkut's son, King Chulalongkorn, the first Thai monarch to travel abroad and as dedicated as his father to the idea of modernisation. An early trip was to Penang, Singapore and Java, where the king was sufficiently impressed by the splendour of British and Dutch colonial buildings to emulate some of them within the Grand Palace as well as nearby. Foreign architects, mainly Italian and British, were called on to execute the designs, which generally reflected those popular in Europe at the time—massive structures with domes, Romanesque facades and elaborate masonry—though sometimes with an unexpected touch of Thai style.

The Chakri Throne Hall, for instance, the first major addition to the Grand Palace compound since its founding, was planned by its British designer as a wholly European building surmounted by three domes. During construction, the king decided to replace the domes with Thai-style spires, resulting in a hybrid that managed to proclaim its progressive spirit while still harmonising with the classic structures surrounding it. Behind the Throne Hall was the Inner Palace, closed to most outsiders and inhabited solely by young boys below the age of puberty as well as queens, concubines, attendants and unmarried princesses from former reigns, who were forbidden to leave the palace compound. Here, too, in a centre of traditional beliefs, there was a new passion for Western style residences with pillared verandahs, rooftop terraces, spiral staircases and occasional whimsical touches like false chimneys.

In 1884, an ambitious 32-year-old Dane named H. N. Andersen bought a small hotel on the river called the Oriental, which catered mostly to visiting seamen. Andersen believed the time had come for Bangkok to have a proper hotel, as opposed to the rather rowdy establishments that then went by the name, and to this end he hired an Italian architect to come up with something to rival those of neighbouring ports like Singapore and Penang. The new Oriental opened three years later with an imposing facade on the Chao Phraya, public rooms that boasted Brussels carpets, French wallpaper, couches upholstered in peacock-blue velvet and a restaurant presided over by a chef named Troisoeufs, who had formerly been in charge of the kitchen at the French legation.

By the early years of the present century, few Thais of means lived in a traditional house, especially in Bangkok and provincial capitals like Chiang Mai. The leading fashion was for multi-storeyed Victorian structures of often complex design and decoration: turrets and oddly-shaped

BELOW **The Author's Wing of the Oriental Hotel in Bangkok, the oldest remaining section, with detail of a carved vent that helped cool the rooms in the days before air conditioning.**

windows, widow's walks, capacious verandahs, stained glass and a lavish application of intricately carved fretwork. Royal palaces, appropriately, were the most elaborate. One, known as Vimarn Mek—a honey-coloured creation overlooking a pond of deep jade-green—was built by Chulalongkorn near the end of his rule and is reputed to be the largest teak dwelling in the world. Phraya Thai Palace, where the king's principal queen moved after his death, had a five-storey tower with verandahs on two floors and a large open audience hall that could seat up to 500 people. When it was turned into a deluxe hotel for a brief period in the late 1920s, tea dances were held in the hall and guests were treated to performances of Thai classical dance in a Greek pavilion in the garden. The greatest concentration of such buildings was to be found in the Dusit District, the most fashionable residential area for members of the royal family, but as the city expanded and roads began to lead away from the old centre, others rose in what were formerly regarded as the distant suburbs.

The simpler bungalow style described by Dr Bradley was popular with foreign residents of the capital as well as among the teak *wallahs* who were settling in Chiang Mai, then a journey of several weeks from Bangkok by boat and elephant back. These were sizable houses, often raised on columns, with deep, cool verandahs, large rooms and French windows looking over equally spacious gardens. In the sleeping quarters, the bed was often placed in the centre and surrounded by what was called a 'mosquito house', amounting to a little room made of mesh. The kitchen was usually separate, as were quarters to accommodate the numerous servants

who took care of the compound and its residents.

Other styles, too, appeared on the scene in the reign of Chulalongkorn's Oxford-educated successor, King Vajiravudh, who built a number of houses that resembled Swiss chalets, Tudor cottages and a curious but effective blend of Gothic and Moorish; one of the latter currently serves as the office of the Prime Minister. The British Embassy shocked some but showed prescience by moving to a new location far from the river, where it assumed residence in a group of solid whitewashed brick buildings containing huge rooms with high ceilings, similar to many colonial edifices throughout the Empire. The property was acquired from a prosperous merchant named Nai Lert who—even before there were roads leading out to the district—had laid out a park on the bank of Klong San Saeb and built a large, multi-roofed weekend home of Burmese inspiration, almost without walls except for the bedrooms.

Different from one another as these foreign-style dwellings were in appearance, whimsical as some of them seem in today's context with their ornate and elaborate architectural flourishes, most shared an important characteristic. They were built for life in a tropical climate in the days before air-conditioning. Keeping cool was a major consideration and it was usually achieved through lofty rooms, verandahs, numerous doors and windows, vast gardens with lily-filled ponds and shady flamboyants, tamarinds and rain trees. In this sense they can be seen as natural successors to the traditional Thai house, which had met a similar need with its raised platform and living quarters arranged to catch every available breeze.

ABOVE *(both)* **Elaborate wood fretwork and louvred shutters were common features in many buildings such as the palace of the Prince of Phrae.**

Vimarn Mek

Vimarn Mek was designed by a son of King Chulalongkorn. The original plan was to build the palace on the island of Si Chang in the Gulf of Thailand, but the incomplete structure was moved in 1900 to Bangkok's Dusit District, not far from the Western-style Throne Hall. The king lived in Vimarn Mek for a few years before moving to Dusit Palace, after which it served as the residence of several royal ladies until his death in 1910. The palace was restored by Her Majesty Queen Sirikit as part of the celebration of Bangkok's Bicentennial in 1982 and is now open to the public.

Built entirely of teak—supposedly the largest teak structure in the world—Vimarn Mek is a rambling collection of interconnected rooms with spiral staircases leading to the upper floors. The top floor was reserved for the king and contains an imported weighing machine, a large copper bath and the first shower ever seen in Thailand.

OPPOSITE *(left)* **A view of the exterior of Vimarn Mek;** *(right)* **One of the palace's many public rooms. The palace was largely empty when Queen Sirikit set about the task of restoring it, and she drew upon the royal family's large collection of furniture and decorative items to accurately reflect the period in which it was built. Most of these were European, though some were especially ordered to meet Thai tastes of the time. Old photographs of King Chulalongkorn and his family adorn the walls.**

THIS PAGE **More public areas of Vimarn Mek.**

OPPOSITE **Exterior view of the octagonal structure of the palace.**

LEFT TOP **The king's study, furnished with a variety of items acquired on his trips to European capitals during his long reign.**

LEFT BOTTOM **The Throne Hall, with seats bearing the royal insignia. On the wall behind hangs a portrait of King Chulalongkorn.**

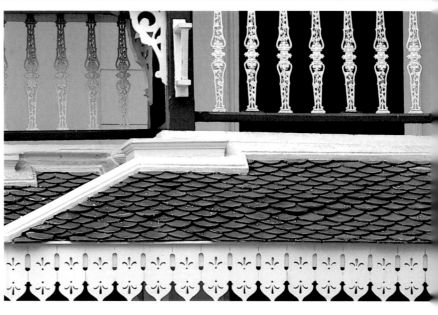

Spacious Quarters

During the first half of Bangkok's history, all the foreign legations were located on or near the busy Chao Phraya, making it easy for representatives to go up by launch on official business to the Grand Palace. The French Embassy residence—built in the middle of the 19th century and gradually added to over the years—is the second oldest remaining today. The building faces the river, with a lawn leading down to the water, and in the style of the day has a broad verandah and living quarters on the upper floor, affording maximum air circulation as well as protection against floods.

Also shown on these pages are details of several other houses in the neighbourhood of the embassy, which was then regarded as a prime residential site for Europeans. The houses are elaborately decorated with Victorian fretwork and follow the same general architectural style as the French residence.

OPPOSITE **Decorative details on several old houses in the vicinity of the French Embassy. All are wood except for the wrought iron balustrades on the lower right.**

ABOVE **A view of the French Embassy from the Tower Wing of the neighbouring Oriental Hotel.**

BOTH PAGES **Views of the verandah of the Tofield house. Rattan furniture and potted plants add to the feeling of airy coolness.**

On the Verandah

The rented home of Anne and Tom Tofield was built around 1910 on Upper Sathorn Road, an area then just becoming popular for residential purposes, especially among Bangkok's foreign community, even though it was far from the commercial centre along the river. Large rooms and breezy verandahs overlooking cool gardens were characteristic of nearly all the European-style houses built during this period. Many have now been air-conditioned and some, like this one, stand in the shadow of modern office buildings. However, they still preserve the old sense of spacious and tropical living in the centre of the city.

An Old House in Thonburi

The Western-style house shown on these pages was constructed in several stages, the earliest towards the end of the reign of King Rama IV; further additions and alterations were made during the next two reigns. A Thai aristocrat named Phya Vichitnavee, who lived there from 1867 to 1923, studied abroad and was associated with the Royal Thai Navy; the house is located on Klong Mon in Thonburi, not far away from the naval headquarters on the Chao Phraya River.

At the time these pictures were taken, the house was unoccupied and the furnishings shown were brought in. Since then it has been rented and extensively restored by Ms Pia Pierre, an antique dealer who uses it as both a residence and as a showcase for her collection.

OPPOSITE (top) **The front of the house. Built around the middle of the 19th century, the house is located on Klong Mon in Thonburi, across the river from Bangkok;** (bottom) **Detail of desk in the sitting room. The design is taken from samples of woodcarving from an old Thai bed.**

LEFT AND BELOW **Views of the upstairs sitting room. The furniture consists of reproductions by Pure Design. Louvred shutters allow air to be freely circulated in the room.**

The Oriental

One of Bangkok's landmarks, the Oriental Hotel was built on the site of an older structure bearing the same name. It used to face the river and consists of a central building with opulently furnished public rooms and long wings that contained the guest rooms. A few years after its opening in 1887, King Chulalongkorn (Rama V) himself came down by royal launch from the Grand Palace to view its much-discussed amenities.

OPPOSITE **The Author's Wing. A double staircase leads to suites named after famous writers, among them Somerset Maugham and Noel Coward.** ABOVE **Exterior view of the Author's Wing, which faces the Chao Phraya River. Note the hotel's original pediment at the top.**

The hotel has been modified a number of times, particularly since the Second World War, with the addition of two new wings in modern style. The oldest remaining section, called the Author's Wing, contains suites decorated in traditional styles and named after noted writers who have stayed at the hotel, as well as a lobby that preserves the atmosphere of the late 19th century even though it is largely the work of contemporary designers.

OPPOSITE *(top)* **Silk wall coverings decorated in traditional Thai designs line the Noel Coward Suite;** *(bottom)* **Another suite in the Author's Wing of the Oriental, the only section remaining of the original hotel.**
LEFT **A table set for a private dinner party in one of the elegantly-furnished reception rooms in the Author's Wing.**
ABOVE **Period furnishings preserve the 19th-century charm in this part of the Author's Lounge. The painting shows the hotel as it looked when it opened in 1887.**

171

ABOVE (*left*) **Shutters of the 19th-century wooden house have been carefully restored and repaired;** (*right*) **Facade of the same house. The tower contains the main staircase.**

OPPOSITE **Main room of the old wooden house, with European-style lounge chairs and table in a style popular during the time when it was built.**

An Evocation of the Past

The former residence of Gerald Pierce, head designer for the Jim Thompson Thai Silk Company, consists of three separate houses set in a beautiful garden that combines both formality and tropical luxuriance.

One, dating from the late 19th century, is a large wooden structure that was moved from its original site in Bangkok and reassembled on one side of the property. Elevated from the ground, the huge central room has the lofty ceilings, shuttered windows and airy quality characteristic of many homes of the time. The other two houses are new but also structured in a spacious style that evokes the past, employing old wooden shutters and carved vents above doors and windows. A kitchen that was once used for entertaining has windows on three sides to provide views of the garden and of a tiled patio sheltered by a vine-covered trellis.

The property was sold several years ago to one of Thailand's leading pop stars, who was so captivated by its atmosphere he also acquired many of the original furnishings.

ABOVE The guest bedroom contains an old Thai bed, baskets and a step in the form of a carved wooden tiger from northern Thailand.

RIGHT View of two of the houses and the garden. The clipped hedges are Ficus trees.

OPPOSITE The kitchen and dining area. The table is an old Chinese altar, while the wooden birds and lacquer receptacles are from northern Thailand.

Petchaburi Palace

Petchaburi Palace, popularly known as Khao Wang, the 'Mountain Palace', was built in the mid-19th century by King Mongkut (Rama IV) as a place where he could relax from his duties in Bangkok and also indulge his passion for astronomy. Having already added several Western-style buildings to the Grand Palace, he followed the same trend in most of the neo-classical buildings that comprise the complex, located at various levels on a hill in Petchaburi province with panoramic views of the surrounding countryside and the Gulf of Thailand.

In a series of ramps flanked by *nagas*, or sacred serpents, a path leads up the hill through masses of gnarled old plumeria trees that provide a welcome fragrance when in bloom. Besides the Western-style buildings with columned arcades and an observatory where the king studied the stars, there is also a more traditional Buddhist chapel and, at the summit, a classic white *chedi* rising against the sky.

The palace was seldom used after the king's death and gradually fell into what one visitor described as "a sad state of neglect". In more recent years, however, it has been beautifully restored by the Fine Arts Department and its original charms are once more apparent.

OPPOSITE **A guard house in the courtyard of Petchaburi Palace, surrounded by blooming plumeria trees.**

BELOW **The view from this palace terrace looks out over the Gulf of Thailand. In the background can be seen the Buddhist temple and *chedi* as well as the king's observatory.**

Hotels and Resorts

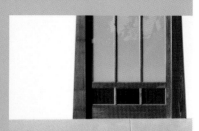

With so many examples of Thai style to draw from, it is not surprising that numerous hotels and resorts throughout the country now make use of its distinctive architectural and decorative features.

Perhaps the first hotel to incorporate recognisable Thai features in its design was the government-owned Erawan, built in the mid-1950s at a busy intersection in central Bangkok. Aesthetically, the effort was something of a muddle, consisting mainly of a few Thai-style touches added to the roof lines of an otherwise purely Western building and assorted decorations scattered around the public rooms to remind guests of the local culture. But for its time, it was regarded as a novelty as well as considerably more luxurious than the venerable Oriental Hotel on the river. (It is worth noting that the Erawan was the hotel of choice for many distinguished visitors, among them Somerset Maugham on his last trip to Asia, who came during the first 10 years or so of its operation. It has since been torn down and replaced by a structure with Greco-Roman columns.)

This tentative effort, sometimes rather hopefully

called 'contemporary Thai', is still to be seen here and there, generally on semi-official buildings like theatres and museums. Whatever impact it may have had, however, has been overshadowed in the last few decades by a dramatic expansion in creations that achieve a more genuine fusion of Thai and contemporary elements. In Bangkok, Chiang Mai, Phuket, Hua Hin, Koh Samui and other places popular with tourists, numerous hotels and resorts now display a wide range of traditional structures and designs that have been acclaimed all over the travel world.

Both Thai and foreign architects have been involved in this continuing process, drawing their inspiration from a variety of sources. The classic Thai house, for instance, has been adapted as a model for striking guest bungalows, sometimes in clusters and sometimes standing alone, overlooking pristine beaches, rice fields and mountain scenery. Similarly, the distinctive Thai multi-tiered roof has been employed on open, pavilion-like structures that serve as lobbies, function rooms and restaurants. Interior designers, too, have made imaginative use of the rich talents of artisans skilled in such arts as woodcarving, sculpture, textiles, painting and a host of others to produce a memorable Thai atmosphere that goes beyond mere decoration.

Not surprisingly, many of the best of these have appeared far from the confusion of Thailand's sprawling capital city. On the island of Phuket in the far south, for example, which was only discovered by tourists in the 1970s, noted architect and developer M. L. Tri Devakul designed a reception hall and a restaurant for the Club Mediterranee with soaring

Thai roofs and the open, airy quality common to traditional structures. This was Phuket's first real resort, opening on Kata Beach in 1986, but it was by no means the last; today new ones seem to open annually, nearly all with Thai themes. M. L. Tri has been responsible for a number, among them the Phuket Yacht Club, Le Meredien, Trisara and two boutique hotels of his own, Mon Tri's Boathouse and the Villa Royale.

One of the earliest resorts opened by the famous Aman group was the Amanpuri on Phuket, designed by the American architect Ed Tuttle. Thai style is predominant throughout, from the luxurious villas offering panoramic views of the sea down a steep hillside to open pavilions for various public rooms, not to mention a profusion of Thai art objects both old and new.

A more recently developed holiday island is Koh Samui in the Gulf of Thailand. It, too, has become the site of a growing number of spas and boutique hotels that incorporate traditional forms of architecture and design. Closer to Bangkok on the west coast of the gulf is Hua Hin, long a favourite seaside resort for members of Thai aristocracy—the royal family has a villa there—but now attracting an international clientele to such retreats as the Chiva-Som, a health spa consisting almost entirely of Thai-style structures.

The hills and mountains of the far north, where cool weather prevails in the winter season, has seen a similar increase in hotels that reflect local culture, which in many ways is different from that of the central region. Two of the most stunning are the Four Seasons Resort, which spills down the slope

of a picturesque valley about an hour's drive from Chiang Mai, and the lavish Mandarin Oriental Dhara Dhevi, virtually a textbook collection of Lanna Thai, Burmese and Lao style structures, nearly 150 in all, built mostly of teakwood on a site covering 21 hectares.

Even Bangkok, a city of towering skyscrapers, shopping malls and miles of undistinguished row shops, has been influenced by the trend. The Sukhothai Hotel, for example, also designed by Ed Tuttle, achieves an atmosphere that is both minimalist-modern and also, through countless subtle features, distinctively Thai. Other hotels, more international in outward appearance, have also created courtyards, lofty terraces, spas, restaurants and even rooftop spaces where guests can enjoy a traditional experience.

Thai style, in other words, has been recognised as a powerful asset in contemporary architecture, especially in places aimed at attracting visitors who want more than just a comfortable place to stay.

PAGE 178 **The Four Seasons Resort in Chiang Mai.**

OPPOSITE **Chiva-Som, a retreat at Hua Hin in the Gulf of Thailand, where an international clientele comes for both traditional and the newest health treatments in a serene Thai setting.**

ABOVE **Le Meredien on Karon Beach in Phuket, designed by architect M. L. Tri Devakul, features a variety of distinctively Thai architectural features.**

BELOW **Panoramic view of the guest rooms, suites and villas from the top of the hill, looking down to the beach and the blue waters of the Gulf of Thailand.**

OPPOSITE **The infinity pool. From here, one can see the mountainous islands of the Ang Thong Marine National Park in the distance.**

Le Royal Meredien Baan Taling Ngam

Located on the western coast of Koh Samui, an idyllic island in the Gulf of Thailand, overlooking the sea and the Ang Thong Marine National Park, this hotel was originally designed by the studio of M. L. Tri Devakul, who was responsible for so many of Phuket's famous resorts. Although it has been altered and renovated a number of times, it has retained the Thai features that helped make it one of the island's most popular retreats. The resort is built down the side of a hill and consists of deluxe guest rooms and suites, as well as beach and cliff villas with one to three bedrooms. All these, as well as the hilltop lobby and restaurants, offer panoramic views of both the sea and the lushly-planted tropical gardens. An infinity pool seems to spill over into a grove of coconut palms below, with an architectural accent provided by a graceful Thai-style pavilion. There are also six other pools in various parts of the property as well as a health spa. Thai furniture, textiles and louvred wood panelling enhance all the guest rooms.

The Sukhothai Hotel

Centrally located on Bangkok's Sathorn Road, the Sukhothai is a surprising oasis of serenity in the busy capital, thanks in part to its setting in 2.4 hectares of gardens and reflecting pools. This, combined with low-rise buildings designed by the American architect Ed Tuttle and an understated interior elegance that manages to be both cutting-edge modern in terms of amenities and distinctively Thai in mood, has made it a particular favourite with business visitors to the capital.

Notable features include pagoda-like *chedis*, inspired by those of ancient Sukhothai, that rise evocatively from a reflecting pool off the lobby, subtly illuminated in the evening; shimmering panels of Thai silk, specially woven for the hotel, on walls and columns; and a collection of strategically-placed terracotta bas reliefs and statues which, though contemporary, are replicas of 14th-century temple decorations. The modern furnishings and the handwoven silks were produced by Chantaka Purananda of Pure Design, while many of the antiques that adorn the various rooms are from the Neold Collection.

Outside the main building, surrounded by ponds of pink and white lotus, is a temple-like structure housing the Celadon, the hotel's Thai restaurant, which is noted for the classic quality of its food. Replicas of blue-green celadon, one of Sukhothai's most celebrated exports, are used in the service here.

OPPOSITE **The lobby of the Sukhothai. The furniture is upholstered in Thai silk. The two terracotta frames, replicas of Khmer gateways, were made in Chiang Mai by an artist atelier named Phor Liang Meun.**

ABOVE LEFT ***Chedis*, pagoda-like structures that are one of the basic Buddhist symbols, stand in a reflecting pool.**

ABOVE RIGHT **The lofty reception hall, with a modernistic flower arrangement by Sakul Intakul and columns covered in hand-woven silk.**

OPPOSITE **The Royal Suite, with silk-covered furniture and antiques chosen for their elegant shapes and simplicity.**
ABOVE **Bedroom of another suite. The ceramics in the niche are of the Sukhothai period.**

Chiva-Som

At Chiva-Som, an internationally acclaimed health spa at the royal resort of Hua Hin on the west coast of the Gulf of Thailand, Thai style can be seen in its simplest, most restrained form. Guest quarters and open pavilions have the classic steep tiled roofs and the graceful curved bargeboard ends but are otherwise free of any unnecessary adornments. The extensive gardens display this same, almost austere quality, with high stone walls, shrubs clipped into topiary shapes, mostly white, fragrant flowers and only an occasional flourish of colour provided by a pot of bright bougainvillea. There are a number of cool, reflecting pools and a few decorative touches like terracotta figures of Hindu gods and goddesses and large, plain water jars—all these enhance rather than disturb the prevailing atmosphere of peace and serenity.

OPPOSITE **Clipped shrubs and meticulously tended lawns line pathways that lead to guest houses at Chiva-Som.** BELOW **The spa is an oasis of serenity. Here, an image of a Hindu deity sits in a reflecting pool, flanked by plants in earthenware containers.**

RIGHT TOP **The Chiva-Som swimming pool. The smaller Thai pavilion on the left serves as a towel rack, while the larger one is used for morning exercises as the sun rises over the Gulf of Thailand.**

RIGHT BOTTOM **Mounted on blocks of clear plexiglass, classic water jars seem to float on the surface of a pool. The terracotta image set in a niche in the wall adds to the atmosphere of serenity.**

OPPOSITE **High stone walls help create a sense of privacy throughout the resort. Note the classic steep tiled roofs and curved bargeboard ends.**

Banyan Tree Phuket

Voted the world's best spa resort by Conde Nast Traveller magazine, the Banyan Tree Phuket is part of a complex of luxury hotels built on the site of an old tin mine. Over 300 million dollars was invested in cleaning the soil and replanting it to create the lush gardens. Each of the Banyan Tree's 109 villas is furnished with locally crafted items and each has its own private garden and sunken, open-air bath.

OPPOSITE **A private pool of one of the spa villas. The multi-armed stone figure on the left is that of a Hindu god.**

ABOVE *(top)* **A lap pool reflects the rich furnishings of a villa;** *(bottom)* **A guest room at the resort, with furniture made of teakwood and wicker.**

Amanpuri—Thai Style on the Sea

The Amanpuri, which overlooks the Andaman Sea on the island of Phuket, is one of the most successful illustrations of how traditional Thai architecture can be adapted to modern uses, in this case an exclusive resort offering privacy to guests. The main part of the resort consists of a series of reception pavilions. Each of the guest rooms is a separate Thai structure built on a steep hillside. Above the resort is a group of privately owned villas designed in the same distinctive style.

OPPOSITE **The resort's black-tiled swimming pool and multi-roofed pavilion.**

THIS PAGE *(both)* **Views of the reception area at the resort. Guests are greeted with the lavish use of wood and the simple but elegant lines of classic Thai style.**

FOLLOWING PAGES **The swimming pool terrace of a villa. Existing coconut palms have been incorporated into the structure. A classic Thai pavilion offers panoramic views of the Andaman Sea.**

RIGHT **Steps lead down the hillside to the beach, shaded by some of the coconut palms already growing on the site.**

BELOW *(left)* **Interior of one of the pavilions. The standing figure is a replica of a Khmer original while the elaborate woodcarving that surrounds it was once the frame of an old door;** *(right)* **Pavilions in the vicinity of the poolside area.**

OPPOSITE **The black-tiled main swimming pool overlooks the Andaman Sea.**

Mandarin Oriental Dhara Dhevi

Covering some 21 hectares just outside Chiang Mai, the recently-opened Mandarin Oriental Dhara Dhevi is an extraordinary tribute to classic Lanna Thai and Burmese styles of architecture and decoration, with additional touches of 19th-century colonial. Notable features include the Dheva Spa, a spectacular recreation of the ancient royal palace in Mandalay with a seven-tier lobby; a collection of Grand Deluxe villas, each in a self-contained compound; a huge free-form swimming pool that wanders through the gardens; and a working rice field at the heart of the property. Fully-grown trees were moved to the site to create the enormous tropical garden.

OPPOSITE **An old fashioned horse-drawn carriage awaits guests by the gate. The octagonal building is a replica of a Shan pavillion.**

TOP **One of several pavilions from which guests can enjoy views of working rice fields over morning coffee or afternoon drinks.**

BOTTOM **This water feature was inspired by the wells in the villages of Tai people in Sip Song Panna, southern China.**

OPPOSITE **Mature stands of golden bamboo and the mellow hues of bricks and teakwood tiles lend a village-like atmosphere to the compound.**

LEFT TOP **A simple yet elegantly furnished bedroom of a villa, with teak walls and a gracefully curving ceiling.**

LEFT BOTTOM **Panelled teak walls and a private jacuzzi combine a traditional atmosphere with modern amenities in this guest room.**

The Anantara Resort, Hua Hin

Originally opened as the Royal Garden Village some 15 years ago, this was one of the first properties displaying Thai architectural features to be built at the popular seaside resort of Hua Hin on the Gulf of Thailand. It has since become part of the Anantara group, with renovated facilities that include a sybaritic spa, but has retained the spacious tropical gardens and traditional atmosphere that made it so distinctive.

The buildings were designed by Thai architect Chulathat Kittibutr, while the landscape and many of the decorative features were created by the Bensley Design Group, which has been responsible for many of the region's most noted resorts. Bill Bensley, who heads the group, has a penchant for dramatic tropical plants, evocative lighting at night and striking artefacts made by local craftsmen, and all these are very much a part of the Anantara's appeal.

Numerous species of palms and flowering trees, shrubs and creepers—over a hundred different kinds in all—fill the garden with colour and varied leaf forms and thanks to a series of ponds, water is an ever-present, soothing feature. Thai-style pavilions and guest rooms are scattered around the large site, which is also adorned with statuary, water jars and other reminders of the culture.

OPPOSITE **The open Thai-style pavilions in the resort's spacious gardens are impressively illuminated at night.**

ABOVE **One of the resort's several restaurants, designed by architect Lek Bunnag and decorated in soothing earth colours.**

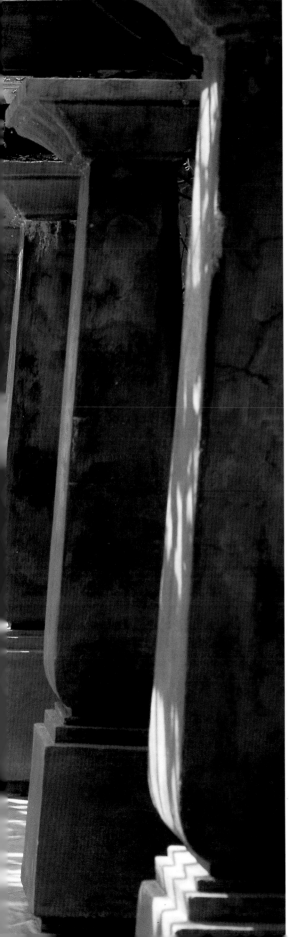

OPPOSITE **A dramatic colonnade with trellises supporting thumbergia, a flower species.**
LEFT **Stone elephants flank a landing overlooking a pond at the hotel's main entrance.**
BELOW **Guest rooms, all built in Thai style, open out to ponds.**
FOLLOWING PAGES **Set among shady trees and greenery, the resort's lily pond lends a restful atmosphere to the resort.**

207

The Rachamankha, Chiang Mai

Boutique hotels with a limited number of rooms and attentive service have become all the rage in Thailand during recent years. Such facilities offer a greater opportunity to incorporate Thai features than larger ones, as shown in the Rachamankha, which opened in 2005 in the northern capital of Chiang Mai.

A creation of love by two of Thailand's best known designers and architects, the Rachamankha has just 18 superior rooms, four deluxe rooms and one two-bedroom suite, but within this limited space it manages to achieve a memorable fusion of Lanna Thai, Chinese and other artistic traditions.

The basic design was inspired by the *vihan*, or chapel, of Wat Phra That Lampang Luang in

OPPOSITE **The swimming pool of the Rachamankha, reflecting some of the guest rooms.**
LEFT **The entrance courtyard of the hotel leading to the open lobby. Betel-nut palms are planted on either side, while a pair of antique water jars display lotus plants.**
ABOVE **View from the lobby to the entrance courtyard. The lobby is furnished with antiques and locally-made furniture.**

211

RIGHT *(both)* **Corridors of the Rachamankha are lined with a collection of scripture cabinets.** BELOW *(left)* **A guest room, decorated with selected antiques;** *(middle)* **The library;** *(right)* **The entrance to the restaurant.**

Lampang, often described as the most beautiful temple in northern Thailand, and the interior decoration reflects the cultures of China, Laos and Burma, all of which were blended in traditional Lanna style. Nearly all the furnishings—from the Lanna-style door with an ornate handle and wooden bolts to bamboo window blinds and table lamps made from Chinese porcelain—are antiques or reproductions. The restaurant is furnished with Chinese tables, large Lanna lanterns and 19th-century paintings depicting the life of the Buddha. Outside, a small but shady courtyard provides al fresco dining accompanied by northern Thai music. The aim, according to the owners, is to give their guests a genuine Lanna cultural experience even in the heart of contemporary Chiang Mai.

The Central Plains Small Family House

The traditional Central Plains house, made in prefabricated sections, is raised on sturdy pillars and has walls that slant slightly inward, steep tiled or thatched roofs with broad over-hangs and bargeboards with curving ends. A typical small family dwelling has a sleeping room opening onto a covered verandah and an open platform where most social activities take place. The kitchen is housed in a separate unit. The area below the house is used to keep the family animals and, in some, for weaving and other handicrafts.

1 Terrace
2 Verandah
3 Bedroom
4 Kitchen

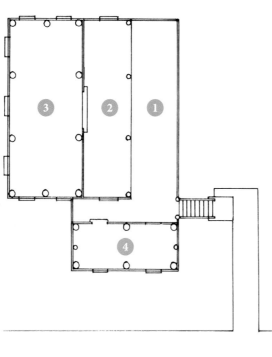

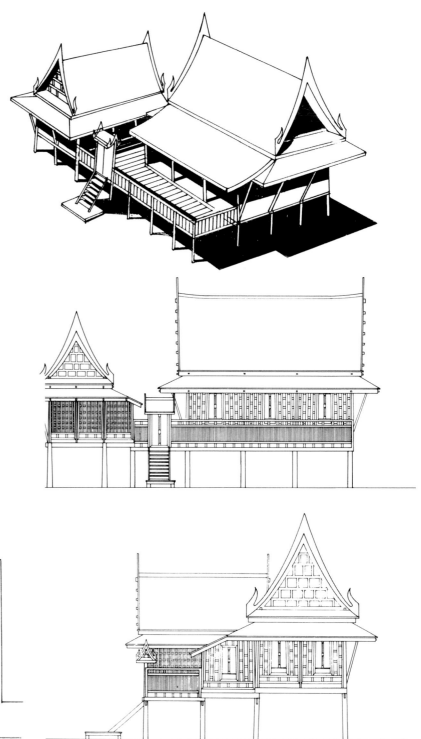

The Central Plains Cluster House

The cluster-type house evolved to meet the needs of extended families who could not be comfortably accommodated in the smaller structures. Several separate sleeping rooms, each with a covered verandah, are arranged around the raised platform, which then serves as a common meeting place. All share the same kitchen and bath facilities. An entrance pavilion where guests are received is often located at the front of the house, at the top of the open staircase. This type of house is subject to numerous variations.

1. Entrance porch
2. Terrace
3. Verandah
4. Bedroom
5. Kitchen
6. Front living area
7. Family area
8. Toilet
9. Bath area

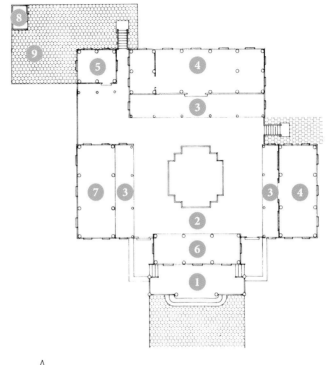

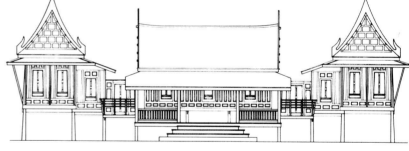

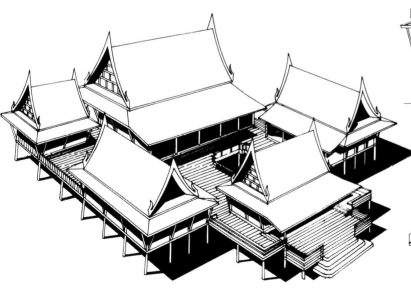

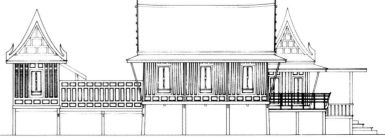

The Northern Thai House

Traditional northern-style houses usually have walls that lean outward towards the roof and smaller windows than those of the central region. Sleeping rooms are sometimes arranged on either side of a corridor as in the example shown here. Decoratively-carved pieces of wood that some have found reminiscent of buffalo horns adorn the roof of the better houses, particularly in the Chiang Mai area. The entire structure is raised on pillars and has an open platform in the front. Shown on this page is the small family house and opposite is an example of the cluster house.

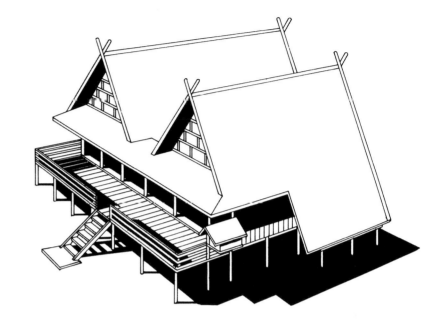

1 Terrace

2 Verandah

3 Bedroom

4 Kitchen

5 Storage

6 Granary

7 Water supply shelf

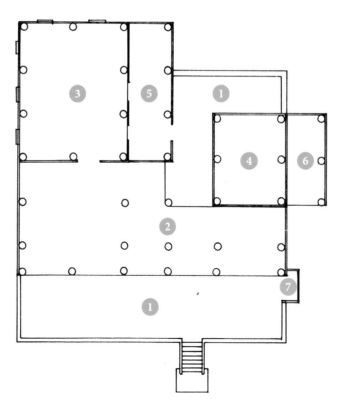

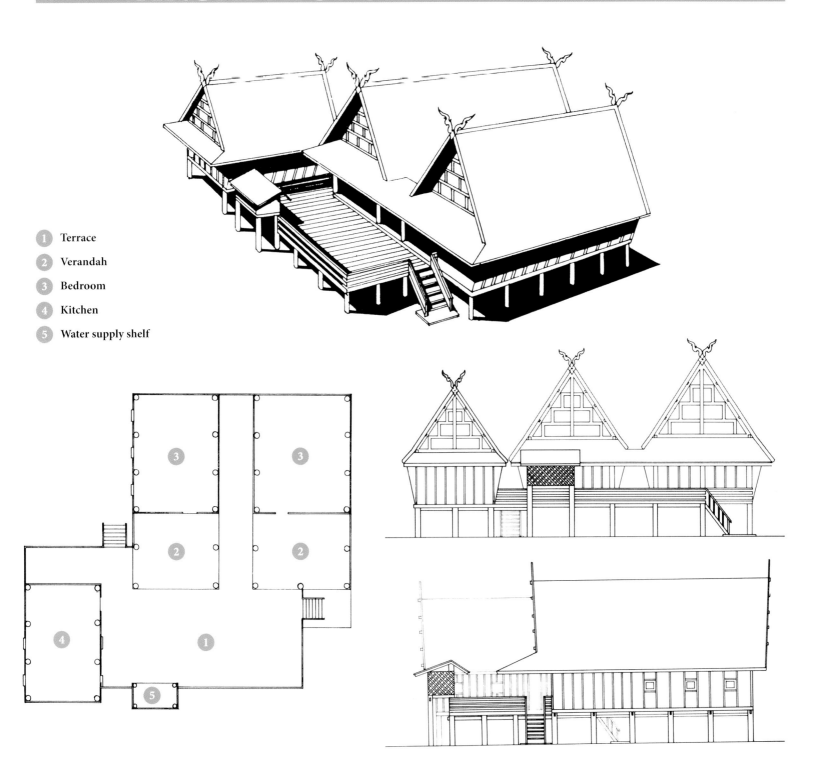

1 Terrace

2 Verandah

3 Bedroom

4 Kitchen

5 Water supply shelf

The bargeboards *(pan-lom)* on the traditional central Thai house have a decorative feature at the end known as *ngao*. This can take many forms, as these examples show, and probably evolved from Khmer temple architecture.

This drawing shows the roofed entrance to a traditional house at the top of the stairway leading to the central platform. A lock for securing the door can be seen on the raised threshold.

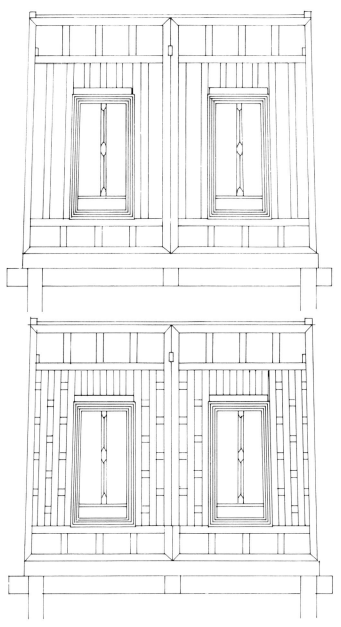

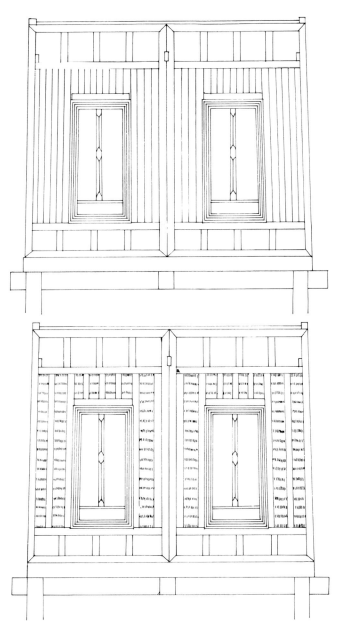

Some examples of panelling on a traditional house, of an elaborate type found in more prosperous homes. Such panelling appears to have been a fairly late development and was a way of using leftover pieces of wood.

The wall in the top drawing is a type found in more common houses where fancy panelling was not used. The drawing below shows the wall of a kitchen with spaces between the boards to allow for more ventilation.

Eave brackets like these support the lower edges of
roofs on temples and royal palaces. They appear in
a variety of forms, among them floral designs and
creatures both mythological and realistic.

222

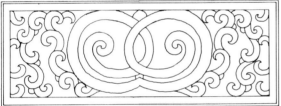

These drawings are examples of designs for *ham yon*, carved wooden lintels placed above the doorway leading into the inner room of a northern house. The symbolic significance of the designs is uncertain, though most of them appeared on numerous houses.

Some examples of the *kalae* decorations found on northern-style houses in Chiang Mai. The exact significance of these is unknown, particularly in more elaborately carved versions like these, but designs often include the traditional flame motif.

Samples of fretwork balcony decorations produced sometimes by hand, sometimes by machine. These became popular in the 19th century and are found on many buildings of the period. The designs are often traditional Thai or Chinese.

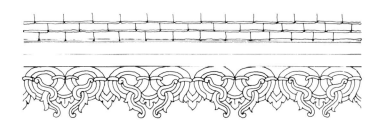

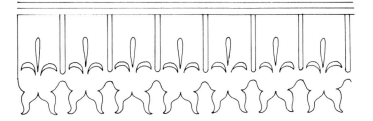

Examples of ornamental strips of fretwork used along the eaves of houses, especially in the 19th and early 20th centuries. Many of the designs reflect traditional Thai motifs.

The drawings show the entrance of an old Chinese shophouse and windows typical of 19th-century Western-style houses with louvred shutters and fanlights.

225

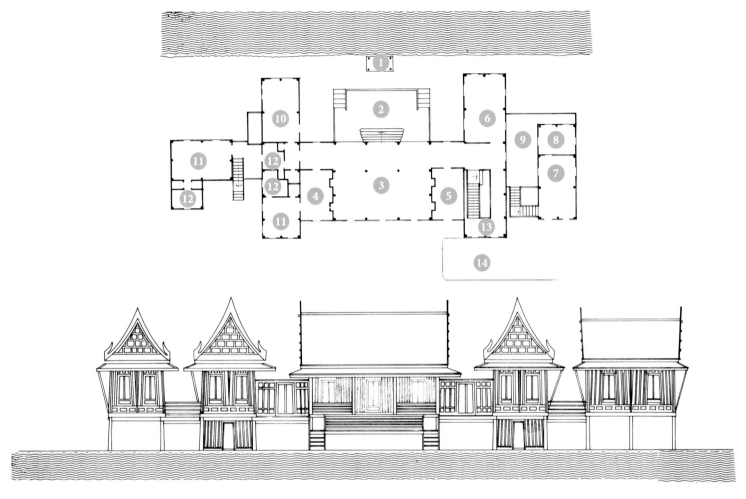

The Jim Thompson House

Architecturally, the Jim Thompson house (featured on pages 94–99) faces Klong Maha Nag and by tradition, guests would have arrived via the *sala*, or open pavilion, on the canal. This being impractical in modern Bangkok, the entrance is through a stairhall at the back. The kitchen and pantry were formed by one of the old houses, while others of varying size were used for the drawing room, the guest room and study and the master bedroom—all joined together in a non-traditional way.

1	*Sala* on canal	8	Pantry
2	Terrace	9	Passageway
3	Drawing room	10	Master bedroom
4	Study	11	Guest room
5	Porcelain display room	12	Bathroom
6	Dining room	13	Entrance stairhall
7	Kitchen	14	Courtyard

Thai-Western Compromise

Privacy was an important consideration in this house (featured on pages 120–123) located in a Bangkok suburb. A canal was dug around the perimeter of the property, which was planted with fruit and ornamental trees and tall stands of bamboo, as well as a number of coconut palms. The guest room is connected to the main dwelling by a wooden walkway.

1 Gate

2 Entrance pavilion

3 Reception pavilion

4 Entrance lobby

5 Living quarters

6 Guest room

7 Kitchen

8 Dining room

9 Living room

10 Music room

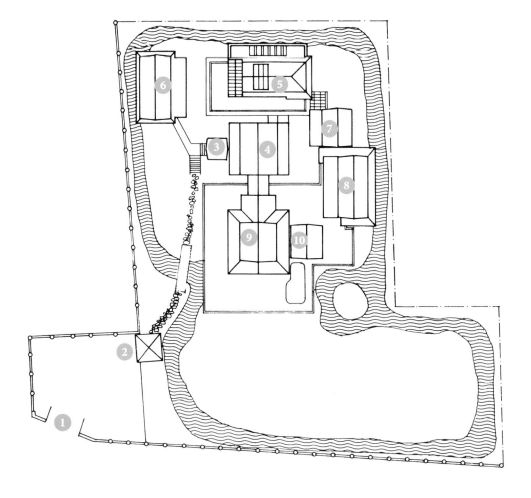

Acknowledgements

This book would not have been possible without the generous assistance of many people, to whom the author and photographer are deeply indebted.

We would particularly like to thank our consultants, Khun Chaiwut Tulyadhan of Neold and Khun Chantaka Puranananda of Pure Design, who introduced us to many homes we would not otherwise have discovered, lent items from their collections to be photographed and devoted many valuable hours of their time to the project; Dr Charlermsri Jan-Orn of Chulalongkorn University, who assisted in the research and provided translations of Thai source material on traditional Thai architecture and Khun Kiatikul Tiyanukulmongkol, who was responsible for most of the architectural drawings of buildings and details.

Our gratitude also goes to all homeowners, as well as managers of hotels and resorts featured, for graciously allowing us to take photographs.

Last, but by no means least, we would like to thank Mrs Gretchen Liu, who provided invaluable support with her editorial skills and wise counsel for the first edition.